The
MEDICINAL
CHEF

Eat your way to
a Healthy Heart

Tackle Heart Disease by Changing
the Way You Eat, in 50 Recipes

DALE PINNOCK

quadrille

CONTENTS

An introduction to
  cardiovascular disease 06
Stress and diet 08
The cardiovascular system:
  what it is and how it works 11
Key physiology 17
The cholesterol conundrum 23
Cardiovascular disease processes 27
The role of nutrition in heart health 34
Key heart-healthy ingredients 52
References, contacts, and resources 58

RECIPES
Breakfast 62
Weekday lunches 71
Weekend lunches 84
Quick dinners 100
Fancy dinners 111
Drinks, desserts, and snacks 127

Index 140

CARDIOVASCULAR DISEASE IS NOW THE BIGGEST KILLER IN THE DEVELOPED WORLD. FACT!

In this day and age you would think that it would be something apocalyptic, such as famine or war, that would be humanity's downfall. But, alas, it seems that in terms of our health, we are the victims of our own "progress."

In the United States, the numbers paint a very scary picture. Someone dies from a heart attack in the US every 33 seconds! More than 920,000 heart attacks are recorded annually and more than 80 million people have cardiovascular disease. This is a staggering statistic. This is epidemic proportions.

In the UK, the situation is also really grim. According to The British Heart Foundation's latest set of released figures, this is the scale of the problem: coronary artery disease will kill one in six men and one in 10 women ... and there are more than 2.3 million people living with the condition in the UK. There are 103,000 heart attacks and 152,000 strokes in the UK each year, while 750,000 people are living with heart failure.

The sad thing is, in these modern times, we are not seeing a decline. In fact, quite the opposite. Heart disease, its deaths, and complications are on a rapid rise and are set to become the leading cause of death on the planet.

Perhaps what is most alarming of all, though, is the fact that the highest proportion of these numbers comes from avoidable circumstances. Granted, there are hereditary factors that can increase our risk of cardiovascular disease but, in the main, we are looking at a lifestyle condition. This means that we really can be in the driving seat here. Of course there are no guarantees in life, but if you don't want to get run over, then jogging blindfolded around the highway is possibly not the best of ideas. Right? Making a few small changes to your lifestyle will be like whipping that blindfold off and getting on the footpath. Something may swerve off the road, but it's fair to say you are doing all you can to stay in the clear.

Our lives today, with their stresses and strains and weird and wonderful habits, are driving the rapid movement toward a cardiovascular epidemic. There are some factors that are really fanning the flames, so let's examine them and see what we can do to help ourselves.

♥ STRESS

Modern life is pretty insane. I think that's a reasonably fair assessment of things. The pressures imposed upon us by this life we have created for ourselves here on 21st century planet Earth are overwhelming. The worries that accompany our financial ebbs and flows are ever growing and, let's face it, listening to the news doesn't help. Juggling home and career is like an insane science. Raising a family. Moving home. Modern life is filled with things that can take their toll on us and cause us to become so far detached from how we are supposed to live.

Now, I'm a realist and I happen to enjoy modern life, so I'm not suggesting you should sell your house, buy a yurt, and set up a commune in California. But learning to manage stress can have a huge impact on many aspects of our health, especially the health of the circulatory system.

Stress can seriously send up our blood pressure, increase inflammation, and play havoc with blood sugar balance. As you will see later in the book, these are important factors in heart health and disease.

♥ DIET

This is where things have taken a massive nosedive. The modern diet in the West doesn't remotely resemble what we are meant to eat. The garbage that has somehow become staple food makes the mind boggle. The consumption of processed food, refined food, fast food, and—frankly—nonfood is off the scale. There are people out there—I speak to a lot of them—who don't eat *any* fruit and vegetables, unless you count beer and fries. This is a serious issue and it affects a big proportion of the population.

There are a lot of others who are trying to be health-conscious and make changes based on outdated and falsified information and guidelines (see page 34). Their good intentions are actually putting them at greater risk of disease.

These factors can be addressed. With a little clarity, focus, and effort, you don't have to become another statistic. We can all move away from this epidemic ... it is not an inevitability.

I will keep the information you need clear and to the point, but I won't skimp on detail. I want you to read this book without getting bored senseless, but also to learn enough from it to understand what is happening in your body, and how the food you eat can directly impact that for good and for bad. Then, best of all, I'll give you inspiration and ideas about how to put this picture all together rather deliciously.

"If you eat the standard Western diet that most people eat in the modern world, it is likely you will develop heart disease."

DR. JOEL FUHRMAN

THE CARDIOVASCULAR SYSTEM: WHAT IT IS AND HOW IT WORKS

Having a basic understanding of the cardiovascular system will enable you to start to build a clear picture of what is going on in your body, how small changes in your diet and lifestyle will have a great impact upon it, and especially how your current diet and changes you make to it may affect your specific issues. "The cardiovascular system" refers to the heart, the blood vessels, and their contents.

THE BLOOD

The most obvious place to start. This tissue is the whole reason the circulatory system exists and finding out what it is, the components in there and which plays what roles will be useful later.

One of the primary functions of the blood is as a transport system. It brings oxygen and nutrients to the cells and tissues of the body. The nutrients we take in—vitamins, minerals, amino acids, fats, glucose, or their by-products—play vital roles in the daily operations of every cell in every tissue in every system. These nutrients and their by-products get where they need to go via the blood. The blood also carries away waste. Our cells are very good at housekeeping; they process waste and throw it out as trash to be carried away in the circulatory system.

The blood is made up of several components:

PLASMA

This is the liquid portion of the blood, and makes up around 55 percent of blood volume. It has very little color—just a subtle pale yellow tinge—and is mostly water with a bundle of proteins, clotting factors, and nutrients suspended in it. It also carries antibodies and other important elements for our immune function.

ERYTHROCYTES

Otherwise known as red blood cells. These are the familiar disklike cells that we often see in images and animations of the blood. Their main job is to transport oxygen to our tissues. Red blood cells contain a protein-based structure called hemoglobin. This is known as a metalloprotein (a protein that binds to metal), as iron makes up an important part of its structure. The iron in hemoglobin actually binds to oxygen to carry it around the bloodstream, where it can be deposited to cells and tissues. This is why people who have serious anemia or iron deficiency become very tired and fatigued, as their capacity to deliver vital life-giving oxygen to cells is diminished. If cells don't get enough oxygen, their ability to create energy and perform many important functions is greatly impaired and severe fatigue and malaise soon set in.

LEUKOCYTES

Otherwise known as white blood cells, these are the second most prominent type of cell in our blood. They are essentially the army of our immune systems, patrolling the body on the look out for anything that is upsetting the peace.

They can rapidly identify invaders that are trying to cause infection or damage. They can also identify our own cells that are suffering for whatever reason. They can tell if one of our cells has become infected and is in trouble. Or they can identify cells that are going through pathological changes, such as the changes that occur during the initiation of cancer. When they make this identification, they can set about a series of events that can deal with it. Some incidents can be dealt with by leukocytes there and then; others may require the leukocytes to recruit help and backup.

There are several different types of white blood cells that do slightly different jobs. I won't go into all the details now but, as we go on, I will touch on the subtle differences as they become relevant to the whole picture of cardiovascular health.

THROMBOCYTES

Also called platelets, these are the third cell type that make up the nonliquid portion of our blood. Their role is to carry out what is called hemostasis. This is basically stopping bleeding at sites of injury. When you cut yourself, the blood doesn't keep oozing out of your body without stopping; we'd soon be in trouble at a very young age if that were the case. This is all thanks to our thrombocytes.

They stop the bleeding by rushing to the area of damage and forming a platelet plug. This is as it sounds, a clumping together of these cells to plug the wound. When this occurs, platelets send out a series of chemical messengers. Clotting factors (substances that assist with the clotting process) that are circulating in the plasma are sensitive to these signals and, when they get to the area of the platelet plug, they begin to lay down a fibrous structure called fibrin, which forms a mesh around the plug and strengthens it.

This series of events is an important thing to remember, as it is a vital part of understanding some of the things that take place in the body in cardiovascular disease.

THE HEART

This astounding pump system is so complex that it is beyond even the best human engineers. There have been numerous attempts to replicate it, all of which have failed miserably. There are artificial systems that can do its job during surgical procedures, but nothing that comes close to mirroring its functionality. About the size of a closed fist, the heart takes the deoxygenated blood (blood that has delivered all of its vital oxygen to the tissues) that is in your veins to the lungs to become oxygenated, before it is taken back off to the tissues of our body once again. It is divided into four chambers: two atria and two ventricles. Between each atrium and ventricle there is a one-way valve that prevents the backward flow of blood, ensuring the pump works as an effective continuous one-way system, with blood flowing in, then out in a perfectly orchestrated fashion.

ANATOMY OF BLOOD VESSELS

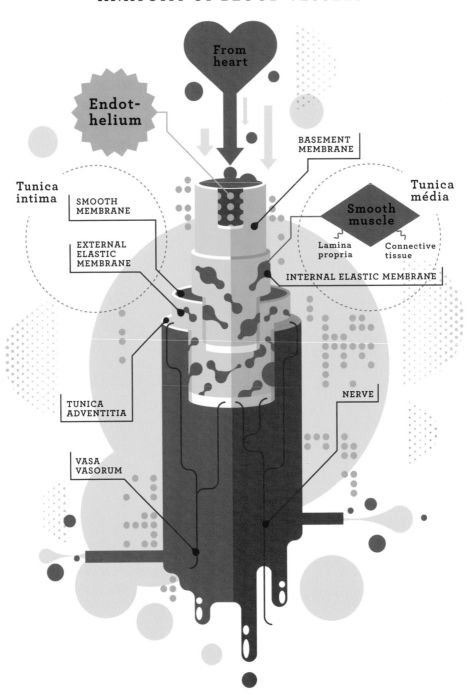

From heart

Endot-helium

BASEMENT MEMBRANE

Tunica intima

SMOOTH MEMBRANE

EXTERNAL ELASTIC MEMBRANE

Smooth muscle

Tunica média

Lamina propria

Connective tissue

INTERNAL ELASTIC MEMBRANE

NERVE

TUNICA ADVENTITIA

VASA VASORUM

The heart is divided in half, with two chambers per half. The right and left sides of the heart have two distinct jobs to do. The right side brings in blood that has low levels of oxygen and sends it to the lungs to get its oxygen levels topped off and also to remove its carbon dioxide. The left side of the heart takes the blood that has been freshly oxygenated and pumps it back out to the rest of the body, sending vital oxygen to our cells.

THE BLOOD VESSELS

Our blood vessels (arteries and so on) resemble a network of incredibly complex plumbing. Thousands of vessels run through our body, some as thick as a hose, others thinner than a single hair, delivering blood, oxygen, and nutrients to our tissues. The thicker ones are called arteries, the next size down are arterioles, with the smallest and finest being capillaries.

Understanding the structure of the blood vessels and how they work is a vital part of understanding the events that take place in cardiovascular disease, and to start seeing how diet and lifestyle may offer both prevention and intervention.

Blood vessels are made up of several layers that all have different functions to carry out. Of these layers, the two I want you to become most familiar with—and those that I am going to discuss most frequently—are the endothelium and the smooth muscle layer.

SMOOTH MUSCLE

The bulk of our blood vessel walls is formed from smooth muscle. Smooth muscle is a type of involuntarily muscle (that means it reacts to environmental and chemical changes, rather than our conscious choice to move it, as we would a muscle in our legs).

Blood vessels need to be incredibly responsive to the constantly changing environment of our bodies and the continual fluctuation in our tissues' needs for oxygen and nutrients. To be this responsive they must change size and shape very quickly.

The smooth muscle in the blood vessel walls can rapidly contract and relax to allow this change to occur. This has great relevance to heart disease as will be described in the next section (see page 27).

ENDOTHELIUM

The endothelium is an incredibly thin yet unbelievably supple and complex inner skin that lines our blood vessels.

At face value level, the endothelium acts as a physical barrier between the blood vessel's contents and the rest of the vessel structure. This in itself is vitally important, as there are many potentially damaging components that can be in our circulation that could affect the health of the vessel.

The endothelium also regulates many aspects of blood vessel function, anything from responding to hormonal signaling to even controlling the activity of the smooth muscle described above. The health of the endothelium is of vast importance to cardiovascular health in general, and will be a recurrent theme in this book.

KEY PHYSIOLOGY

OK, so I'm not going to expect you to suddenly become a heart surgeon or anything, but I do firmly believe that you should be as informed as possible about the inner workings of your body. There are a few aspects of how the cardiovascular system works that will really help you both to start to put the information in this book into some kind of context and to bring the bigger picture together. The more you can grasp what is going on, the better you can understand · how nutrition is a key part of the solution. There are a few main areas, things that you would have heard about over and over—either from your physician or in the news—that are vital to understand. The first of these is:

BLOOD PRESSURE

We all know by now that, if blood pressure is too high, we have a problem. The British Heart Foundation estimates that there could be in excess of five million people in the UK with undiagnosed high blood pressure. That is a serious number. But what *is* blood pressure? What does the term mean and why is it such a big deal?

Blood pressure is basically the pressure that circulating blood places on the blood vessel walls. There has to be a certain amount of pressure in our vessels so that each contraction of the heart can push the blood to where it needs to go. As the blood is moved along, it exerts pressure against the vessel wall. That's it. So, why does it matter how high it is?

The higher your blood pressure is, the more force is placed upon the blood vessel walls, which figures. The vessel walls are designed to withstand a vast amount of force, but not a limitless amount. We get to a point where too much pressure is a problem. If your blood pressure is high enough for long enough, then the vessel becomes more susceptible to damage and any areas that have already been damaged from previous events run the risk of getting worse.

WHAT THE NUMBERS MEAN

When we have our blood pressure checked, we are told (sometimes) a couple of numbers, then there is usually a suggestion as to whether they are good or bad. But what do the numbers mean? Following a blood pressure measurement, you will be told that your blood pressure is "something over something"; 120 over 80 for example. The first number (systolic), represents the pressure exerted on the vessel wall when the heart squeezes and a large volume of blood is forced through the blood vessel. The second (diastolic) number points to the pressure put upon the vessel wall when the heart is at rest, or between beats. So which number is the most important? Well, in most cases it is the first one, the number that shows how much of a beating the vessel wall is taking under the most amount of force. The higher this is, the more risk there is of vascular injury, heart attack, or stroke. More pressure = more chance of damage. (However, according to Blood Pressure UK, recently it has been thought that in those less than 40 years old, diastolic pressure is a greater predictor of risk. This may be because it can show that there is less flexibility in the vessel wall than expected, or that a kind of hardening has started to take place.)

WHAT IS NORMAL AND WHAT ISN'T?

There isn't really a gold standard perfect reading as such, and the old saying that your blood pressure should be 100 plus your age doesn't actually stand up to a lot, but these ranges (see right) should give you a rough idea.

WHAT CONTROLS BLOOD PRESSURE

The main driver of blood pressure is a pair of responses called vasoconstriction and vasodilation. Vasoconstriction makes the vessel get smaller and narrower. Vasodilation makes it get larger and wider. As a vessel constricts and gets narrower, the pressure within it gets much higher, as a specific volume of blood is having

BLOOD PRESSURE

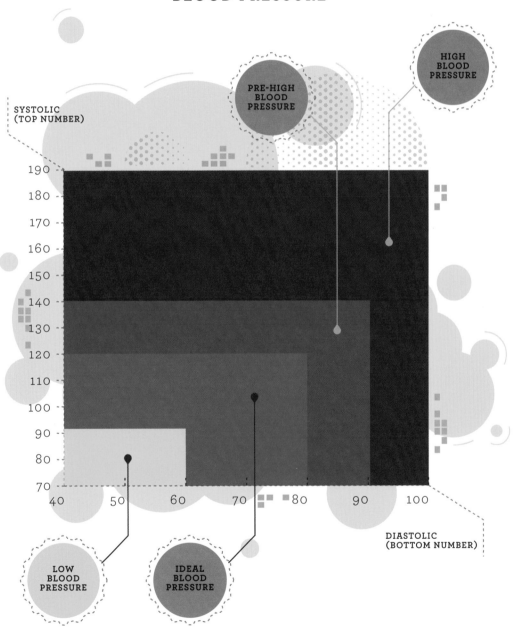

SYSTOLIC
(TOP NUMBER)

PRE-HIGH
BLOOD
PRESSURE

HIGH
BLOOD
PRESSURE

LOW
BLOOD
PRESSURE

IDEAL
BLOOD
PRESSURE

DIASTOLIC
(BOTTOM NUMBER)

"Think about it. Heart disease and diabetes, which account for more deaths globally than anything else combined, are completely preventable by making comprehensive lifestyle changes. Without drugs or surgery."

DR. DEAN ORNISH

to be forced through a smaller space. When a vessel dilates and gets wider on the other hand, the pressure within it drops as there is more space for the blood to fill, hence less force exerted on the blood vessel wall. A healthy vessel is moving between these two states constantly to keep our blood flowing along nicely.

Everything from physical activity to the health of our blood vessels will determine the rate and extent to which these changes occur. In a healthy individual, the move between vasodilation and vasoconstriction should be smooth and highly responsive. If you recall from the previous section (see page 15), the bulk of our blood vessel walls are made up of layers of smooth muscle. This smooth muscle is the key component of the blood vessels that allows them to widen and constrict so readily. The muscle contracts; the vessel gets narrower. The muscle relaxes; the vessel gets wider.

Think back to the previous section and you will recall that I placed great importance on the endothelium, that thin but vitally important inner skin that lines our blood vessels. Well, this seemingly simple structure is one of the major controllers of vasodilation. This is due to a highly active chemical that the endothelial cells produce, called nitric oxide. When the endothelial cells produce nitric oxide, it leaves the endothelial cells and then migrates out deep into the vessel walls, where it encourages the smooth muscle of the blood vessel to relax, which then allows the vessel to widen. Vasoconstriction is caused by a number of chemical factors, from calcium flowing into the muscle, through to neurotransmitters. Calcium, for example, causes muscle fibers to move together and muscles to contract, which in turn will narrow the blood vessel wall.

In terms of how nutrition can influence this whole picture, nitric oxide production and vasodilation is the most relevant part. The section of this book that describes cardiovascular disease processes will give you a good idea of how things can start to go wrong with the endothelium and the knock-on effects of that through the system as a whole, then when we get to explore the role of nutrition in cardiovascular health, we will begin to see how certain nutrients and dietary patterns can influence this. Hopefully, by building the picture piece by piece, you will finish reading the book with a better understanding of what's going on and what you can do about it.

BLOOD CLOTTING

This is a normal and absolutely vital response to injury and, without it, we would be in big trouble. It basically describes a series of events that stem bleeding when a vessel is injured. This can be the obvious type of injury, such as when you cut yourself, or silent internal injuries, such as damage to a blood vessel wall or a ruptured plaque (more on that later).

Sticking with the cut finger, you will realize that, when you cut yourself, you don't carry on bleeding to the point that you turn white and keel over. After a minute or so, the bleeding stops; give it a good few hours and a scab will start to form. This is the whole process of coagulation in action.

When an area of a blood vessel becomes damaged, whether a kitchen knife plows through it or an atherosclerotic plaque ruptures (again, more on that later), a response is set in motion. Thrombocytes (platelets) begin to clump together around the site of injury to form a platelet plug. When this occurs, platelets send out a series of chemical messengers. Clotting factors that are circulating in the plasma are sensitive to these signals and, when they get to the area of the plug, they begin to lay down a fibrous structure called fibrin, which forms a mesh around the plug and strengthens it. This is essentially like a scab; the masking tape over the leak in the hose. A makeshift repair job that stems the bleeding, while your body begins to repair damaged tissues. While this sequence of events is designed to save your life, as we'll see, when the process happens within a blood vessel, there is the potential for it to be life threatening.

THE CHOLESTEROL CONUNDRUM

I don't think there is any greater area of misunderstanding, confusion, contradiction, and outright panic than the area of cholesterol and heart health. So many clients that I have worked with over the years have been almost fixated on their cholesterol levels ... and terrified by the numbers.

Massive health campaigns that cross continents and span generations have been among the public health front runners. There have been TV campaigns, funny little drinks, you name it. And there have been many efforts to get us all to reduce our cholesterol and, of course, many a commercial opportunity, too. But how many of us actually understand our cholesterol, know what it is, or even know what half the terminology means?

Let's get one thing perfectly clear from the start: cholesterol is a vital substance. The fact that our body produces up to one gram of it per day, regardless of what our diet looks like, is a pretty good indicator that it may actually need to be there and may not be the murderous villain that we are led to believe it is. Mechanisms that lead to that scale of production inside all our bodies cannot be some unfortunate physical flaw; they exist because the substance is vital to our health. Cholesterol is needed for the manufacture and maintenance of cell membranes.

Each cell in our body consists of hundreds of different pieces of machinery and a host of biochemical signaling and relaying systems. These substances are held in place by a double-layered fatty bubble called the membrane. The membrane also helps our cells to function, as it actively gets involved in carrying messages from outside the cell to the inside, and moving things in and out. So, all in all, pretty important! Cholesterol helps strengthen the bonds within this structure, so it is more resilient. It also helps to secure specific proteins found within cell membrane walls that are involved in relaying signals between the inside and outside of cells.

Cholesterol plays an incredibly important role in digestion, too, as it is also used to create the bile acids that are released from the liver during digestion. Specifically they are involved in the breakdown of fats into smaller, more manageable particles, ready for absorption. Cholesterol has another vital role to play. It is the metabolic precursor (the chemical building block) for some vital substances in the body. One of the most important is vitamin D.

As you may be aware, vitamin D is the latest nutritional darling and the center of a huge amount of research. What we are discovering about it is truly remarkable. We all know that it is important for maintaining healthy bones, because it helps the body to use calcium properly. But its benefits don't stop there. It has been shown to affect both mind and mood and it also regulates immunological responses.

Where does it come from? Well, a certain amount can come from our diet, from foods such as oily fish and variety foods. But the primary source of vitamin D for humans is the conversion of cholesterol into vitamin D when our skin is exposed to ultraviolet radiation (the sun)! In the UK, the sun is little more than a rumor for most of the year, so if the benefits of what little Brits do get are stifled by having very low levels of vitamin D precursors, we are in a bit of trouble.

Cholesterol is also the precursor for our main sex hormones: estrogen and testosterone. The body needs cholesterol to make these. I don't know about you, but I for one don't want to see my levels of testosterone plummet any time soon! So, with all this in mind, I think it is clear that cholesterol isn't the demonic destroyer of health that we automatically suppose.

LDL AND HDL

I guess you might have heard the terms LDL cholesterol and HDL cholesterol. These are sometimes also called "bad" and "good" cholesterol. What do they mean? Well, to start with, there is only one type of cholesterol. Cholesterol = cholesterol. It is a thick waxy substance. As such, it doesn't mix well with our blood (oil and water just won't mix) so, left to its own devices, it wouldn't get very far or fare very well just bobbing around fattily in our bloodstreams.

To this end, the body has its own transport system to shuttle cholesterol around the body. These are like two different bus routes and the bus is called a lipoprotein, a protein that can give fatty substances a piggy back. LDL = Low Density Lipoprotein, HDL = High Density Lipoprotein. LDL carries cholesterol out into our bodies' tissues via the bloodstream. HDL returns cholesterol from the blood to the liver for recycling and breakdown.

So, the theory goes that if your LDL (bad) cholesterol is high, then you are at greater risk of heart disease, but if your HDL is high, then it's good news. The basic proposition was—for a very long time—that an excess of cholesterol in the blood would begin to deposit itself in the walls of the blood vessels and cause a plaque. It was as simple as that. The more there was, it was thought, the greater your risk of developing heart disease, as more cholesterol would be getting deposited out into your tissues. The resulting medical treatment protocol for the prevention of cardiovascular disease focused upon getting levels of cholesterol down.

For a couple of decades, the medical profession were happily able to target a specific biochemical marker (cholesterol) in an attempt to decrease cardiovascular disease. Very soon there was a multibillion dollar market in pharmaceuticals such as statins, while the functional foods market (those funky little cholesterol-lowering drinks) was also beginning to boom.

But, as the years went by and research moved forward, this clear picture and perfect theory began to fall apart. Did you know that almost 75 percent of people who have a heart attack have clinically "normal" cholesterol levels? Normal, as in at healthy levels … now there's a conundrum! Recent studies have even shown that a large proportion of patients with heart disease have a lower-than-average level of cholesterol. If it were purely a numbers game, then this simply would not be the case. Something else must be going on.

Perhaps we have missed the trick! There are populations on the Earth, such as the Inuit people, that have been shown to have staggeringly high cholesterol levels, yet heart disease in their communities is as good as nonexistent. Is there something else in their environment, diet, or even their genes that offers them protection? If cholesterol were the single pathogenic factor that we have been looking for, then this lack of clarity as well as the seemingly outright contradiction would simply not exist.

CARDIOVASCULAR DISEASE PROCESSES

Heart disease isn't something you just get struck down with. It is the result of a lot of small changes coming together over time. Many of the things that you have heard of as being risk factors for heart disease—such as high blood pressure, or smoking—essentially set the stage for a series of events to occur which can lead to the condition ultimately known as heart disease.

There are several pathological (disease causing) events that take place. There isn't always a specific order for these occurring and, very often, one gives rise to another in a vicious cycle. Here are the main events, the key pathological processes, and certainly the ones that have been at the center of most studies. Understanding them properly will help you get a better grasp on how nutrition and lifestyle can be one of the most powerful parts of your armory against cardiovascular disease.

ENDOTHELIAL DYSFUNCTION

The endothelium, as we have seen earlier in this book, is the skin that lines the inside of our blood vessels. This thin skin is absolutely vital in maintaining the function of the rest of the blood vessel and, when it goes wrong in some way, the consequences can be devastating to cardiovascular health.

And one of the fundamental areas where the endothelium can start to malfunction is when it has a reduced production or utilization or release of nitric oxide. This is a chemical that is naturally made by—and released by—the endothelial cells, and which controls several aspects of vascular biology. It reduces blood clotting, reduces the movement of white blood cells into the vessel walls (see plaque formation, page 30), and also reduces the oxidation of LDL cholesterol. The major and most widely understood role for nitric oxide, however, is vasodilation, which means the widening of blood vessels (remember from when we explored blood pressure, see page 17). This is the relaxation of the muscular walls of the blood vessels. It is normally stimulated mostly by sheer stress placed on the vessel walls by blood flowing through. Nitric oxide is produced and released by endothelial cells in response to immediate localized changes that signal a need for a change in blood pressure or vessel function.

Problems arise when nitric oxide release or utilization is impaired. The first and most obvious consequence is the reduced capacity for the vessels to widen under stress. Lets use the analogy of a hose to give some clarity to this. Imagine you have two hoses. One is made of flexible, responsive rubber, the other of stiff, inflexible plastic. When water runs through them at a normal and steady pace, they both perform perfectly well. But, what happens if you should turn on the faucets at full pelt? The rubber hose, when faced with the sudden rise in pressure, will simply stretch and expand and "go with the flow." The plastic one has no give, so begins to crack and split under the pressure.

Well, this gives you an idea of how things go awry when our blood vessels are less responsive to changes in pressure. Suddenly we are at more risk of damage to the endothelium from the increased pressure against the vessel walls, and any areas of repaired damage and plaques (see page 30) are more susceptible to further damage and rupture. The initial stages of endothelial damage, whether induced by physical stress or other events, involve, and lead to ...

INFLAMMATION

We are now at the point, with research going in the direction that it is, where we can say with certainty that, despite whatever else is going on in the body, cardiovascular disease is essentially an inflammatory condition. Inflammation that causes damage to the vital endothelium and then fuels further pathophysiological changes in the body.

Inflammation is a normal, natural, and vital thing. It aids our immune system in dealing with pathogens, infection, or damaged tissue. In cardiovascular disease, it seems there is a two-way street, or a vicious cycle. Inflammation can cause endothelial dysfunction; endothelial dysfunction can cause inflammation.

One of the main and most widely established causes of inflammation within the endothelium is the oxidation of LDL cholesterol. LDL cholesterol can become damaged by circulating free radicals (reactive oxygen molecules that cause damage) and be readily oxidized (damaged and chemically altered). When this happens, the oxidized cholesterol can cause damage to the endothelium. Oxidation makes LDL far more able to penetrate the endothelium and cause some of the damage outlined over the page (plaque formation). Other factors that can trigger inflammation are smoking, high insulin levels—caused by eating too many fast-release carbohydrates for too long—and stress.

But, probably, the biggest factor of all for most of us in the Western world is the wrong types of fats in our diet. I am going to go into much more detail in the next chapter on nutrition and heart disease and heart health, but in the Western world we are eating too much of a type of fat that may be killing us slowly. Now, before you think this may be that old-school message about saturated fat that you have heard a million times for decades and that has now been proven to be wrong, think again. Listen up: saturated fat is not the villain that you might have thought.

In fact, the wrongdoer was the thing we moved over to when we all began abandoning butter for "heart-healthy" margarines! We are consuming too much of something called omega 6 (see page 34 for more on this). Omega 6 is a polyunsaturated fatty acid that, when metabolized by the body in more than minuscule amounts, actually exacerbates inflammation.

When inflammation arises within the endothelium, the next series of events that can occur are ...

PLAQUE FORMATION

Plaques are the things that form in the blood vessel walls during what is called atherosclerosis. This is what people are referring to when they use the rather crude terminology of "furring up," or "clogging," of the arteries. They are the result of a series of events and knowing some of the stages will allow you to understand those elements of diet and lifestyle that may offer help in the prevention and management of the condition.

The first stage of this process stems from damage to the endothelium, that thin inner skin that lines the blood vessel. This can be susceptible to damage, given the right circumstances (such as those that stem from endothelial dysfunction described on page 27). When this damage occurs, circulating materials in the bloodstream—such as cholesterol and fats—can get trapped in the area of damage. Cholesterol that has become trapped in this area suddenly becomes more susceptible to oxidation and damage, due to the array of chemical responses taking place as all this circulatory junk accumulates. When the cholesterol oxidizes, it triggers an inflammatory response. This then alerts circulating white blood cells, which move to the site of vascular injury. White blood cells, being what they are, wade in and try to help clean up the mess because, after all, this consistent oxidation of cholesterol can cause untold damage if not managed. So, in order to contain this, the white blood cells begin to swallow up oxidized cholesterol.

When white blood cells do this, they begin to change and transform and become what is known as foam cells. When they have changed in this way, their normal ability to move and circulate disappears and they stay put at the site of injury. This is the first stage of what is termed a fatty streak, or fatty buildup within the blood vessel wall.

As this matures, smooth muscle cells from the muscular walls of the vessel also begin to move into the mass of foam cells and aid in supplying a matrix of fibers that can make this fatty streak more stable. It becomes a collection of fatty material, topped with a fibrous cap that is essentially holding everything in place.

This plaque can sometimes be very stable and lay unaffected in the blood vessel for a whole lifetime. At other times, plaques can be very unstable, meaning that the slightest increase in blood pressure, or increased force on the vessel wall from blood flow, can cause the plaque to rupture, which gives rise to a thrombus (see below). Also, chronic inflammation that has built up over a long time can give rise to the release of enzymes that can break down the fibrous cap, again leading to rupture. When this happens, the next stage is ...

THROMBUS FORMATION

When atherosclerotic plaques rupture, a blood clot quickly forms around the site of rupture. This can be likened to the formation of a scab when you cut your finger. When damage occurs, the affected area sends out chemicals that activate platelets in the blood. Platelets are known as cell fragments. They are cells without a nucleus and contain much less complicated machinery than most cells in our bodies.

When the platelets are activated, they become sensitive to the effects of different clotting factors. These varying clotting factors come into play, binding platelets together using a fibrous mesh called fibrin. This ends up almost like a layer of netting that holds everything in place.

This clot can grow quite large, sometimes large enough to completely block the blood vessel it is inside. When this happens, the tissue it supplies becomes oxygen starved. Depending on how long this state lasts, the tissue may lose some of its function, or die completely. This is what is known as infarction.

In a heart attack, this occurs in a vessel that supplies blood to the heart muscle. In a stroke, this happens in a vessel that supplies blood to the brain.

THROMBUS FORMATION

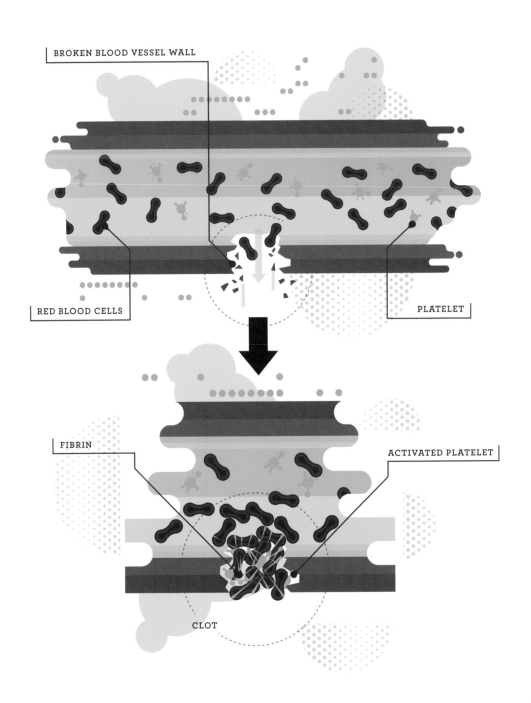

BROKEN BLOOD VESSEL WALL

RED BLOOD CELLS

PLATELET

FIBRIN

ACTIVATED PLATELET

CLOT

Sometimes, the clot forms in a relatively wide blood vessel and is in no way big enough to cause occlusion (blockage) of the vessel. But, with changes in blood pressure and the force exerted onto the blood vessel wall from blood flow, clots (thrombus) can be dislodged. They can then move through the circulatory system.

As the blood vessels get closer to key tissues, they get smaller and smaller and their networks more intricate. As a thrombus moves through this seemingly endless network, sooner or later it will end up reaching a vessel that is just too small to accommodate it, where it will then cause a blockage.

THE ROLE OF NUTRITION IN HEART HEALTH, DISEASE PREVENTION, AND DISEASE MANAGEMENT

It is a certainty that 90 percent of cases of cardiovascular disease are ultimately preventable. That sounds like a bold statement, I know, but one I stand by. They are a result of our environment. This is of course partly the external environment we live in, such as stress, pollution, and so on. But, when we talk of environment, we are referring to the internal biochemical terrain of the body. There is nothing that can influence this biochemical terrain more than our diet. With a few simple changes, we can guide our diet toward being cardioprotective. This means it can support cardiovascular health, potentially prevent the damaging issues, and play a role in the management of any existing cardiovascular issues.

OMEGA 3, OMEGA 6, AND A QUESTION OF BALANCE

Many of you that are familiar with my work will have probably realized by now that I am a little obsessed with dietary fats. It is my belief that the fat composition of our diet is one of the key factors in cardiovascular health and disease. The fixation with dietary fats and cardiovascular health is, however, the reason we have got into such a mess in the first place, with the huge prevalence of this disease globally. In the last four or five decades, the patterns of fat intake in our diet has changed drastically. This is mostly thanks to the work of a man by the name of Ancel Keys.

Keys was an American physiologist who came up with a hypothesis that the cause of cardiovascular disease was saturated fat intake. He was a very ambitious guy and set out to prove this hypothesis with vigor. He designed a 22-country study. It literally was as the name suggests, a study of 22 countries, searching for a correlation between saturated fat intake and cardiovascular disease. Now, the odd thing was, when this study was published, it was as

"The Seven Countries Study"; only seven of the 22 countries' results were used and the results looked very impressive indeed. The data produced a beautiful positive curve and essentially proved Keys's hypothesis that saturated fat intake was indeed associated with cardiovascular disease. But hang on a minute. What about the other 15 countries? What's going on here?

As it turns out, the seven countries selected were those that actually supported his theory. Had Keys used all 22 countries, the data would have shown absolutely no correlation whatsoever between saturated fat intake and cardiovascular disease. What was published was basically a fraudulent and engineered piece of reporting. Selective inclusion and exclusion of data that "proved" something that didn't exist. But, alas, this study was taken on board around the world and Keys became a hero.

Before long he appeared on the cover of *Time* magazine and his misleading study became the inspiration for the biggest public health mess known to man. In no time at all, the American government were developing a public health campaign that encouraged the population to ditch saturated fat and move toward a diet that was high in starchy foods and the supposed "heart-healthy" oils such as sunflower oil and margarine. The same public health message made it to the UK soon after and then began to dominate the Western world. We took it on board. Didn't we just! This is where the problem began.

You can actually see, by looking at data from institutions such as the World Health Organization, that as these changes in our diets occurred and we moved toward more starchy foods and more polyunsaturated oils, the incidence of cardiovascular disease, type-2 diabetes, and cancer began to soar and, all of a sudden, we saw an obesity epidemic.

So, why are these dietary changes an issue? Well, I will talk about the starchy foods in greater detail when I discuss the glycemic effects of foods and their relevance to heart health. But, for now, let's look at the oils that we started to consume in place of saturated fats. The message was that we needed to move toward a higher intake of vegetable oils, so sunflower, corn, and soy oils and spreads became super-popular. Sickeningly they began (and still do) adding the "heart-healthy" label to their products and advertising.

OMEGA 6

The problem that was completely overlooked in those early days was that most vegetable oils are incredibly high in things called omega 6 fatty acids. These are essential fatty acids that are vital to the body and must come from the diet as our body can't make them itself. All good so far. The problem is, however, that we only need a very small and finite amount of omega 6. Once we go over this level, the body metabolizes it in a slightly different way than it would when we are at safe levels and changes it for the worse. Fatty acids in the diet are the metabolic building blocks for several important structures and compounds in the body. One of the big and vital groups that they give rise to are a group of communication compounds called prostaglandins. One of the main roles that prostaglandins carry out in the body—and this is important—is in the management of inflammation.

There are three different types of prostaglandins: Series 1, Series 2, and Series 3. Series 1 are mildly anti-inflammatory. Series 3 are strongly anti-inflammatory, switching off or down and regulating inflammation, and regulating pain signaling. Series 2 prostaglandins, on the other hand, actually switch on and exacerbate inflammation. This isn't a bad thing per se, providing that the body can be in a state of flux and produce sufficient amounts of these compounds to manage inflammation adequately.

But the balance of dietary fats in our bodies can disrupt this process. Different dietary fats are metabolized to form different series of prostaglandins. Omega 6 fatty acids are the metabolic precursors to—you guessed it—the Series 2 prostaglandins that switch inflammation on. The drastic shift in dietary fat intake in the last decades has meant that in the UK they take in almost 23 times more omega 6 fatty acids than we need *per day*!

We are essentially force-feeding metabolic pathways that manufacture prostaglandins, and our body's expression of the proinflammatory Series 2 goes into overdrive. The end result is a state of subclinical (your foot doesn't suddenly swell up, this is happening on a microscopic level within tissues), chronic (consistent and long-term) inflammation in the body. These compounds travel around the body in our circulation, so one of the first tissues to take a battering is, of course, the endothelium, as it is the tissue that is immediately exposed to their changing levels.

If you recall from the previous chapter, inflammatory damage within the endothelium sets the stage for plaque formation and, in essence, cardiovascular disease. The dietary change that was supposed to bring down cardiovascular disease ended up killing us faster. It was akin to trying to put out a bonfire with gasoline.

OMEGA 3
This is the perfect time to bring in the other big dietary fatty acid, one you have probably heard a great deal about: omega 3 fatty acids. The benefits of omega 3 on heart health are well documented and have been studied widely for at least 20 years. These amazing fatty acids are the antidote to what we have just learned. There are three main types of omega 3: ALA, EPA, and DHA. EPA and DHA are metabolized to form Series 3 prostaglandins (EPA more so). These are the most potently anti-inflammatory. So, eating good amounts of omega 3 fatty acids encourages our body to produce more anti-inflammatory prostaglandins.

A growing body of evidence is showing that fish and fish oil consumption appears to offer significant protective benefit against heart disease; indeed, several studies have shown that fish consumption is directly related to a reduced risk of heart disease.

"I'm not comfortable recommending people eat saturated fat with abandon, but it is clear to me that sugar, flour, and oxidized seed oils create inflammatory effects in the body that almost certainly bear most of the responsibility for elevating heart disease risk."

DR. ANDREW WEIL

A review of three large-scale epidemiological studies found that men who ate at least some fish per week had lower incidence of heart disease than those who ate none ①. Similar patterns were also found in women. A 2002 report from The Nurses' Health Study showed that, compared to women who ate no fish, risk of cardiovascular disease deaths were 21 percent, 29 percent, 31 percent, and 34 percent lower for a fish consumption of respectively one to three times per month, once per week, two to four times per week, and more than five times per week ②.

Omega 3 fatty acids have also been shown to reduce levels of triglycerides. These are fats in the blood that can arise from dietary fat intake and from eating very high-GI foods (see page 41). These fats are believed to be very susceptible to oxidative damage, which could cause or aggravate endothelial inflammation and oxidize LDL cholesterol. A 1997 review of human studies found that around 4g per day of marine-derived omega 3 fatty acids reduced triglycerides in the blood by 25 to 30 percent ③.

Postprandial triglyceridemia is the elevation of fats in the blood following a meal. This elevation in triglycerides appears to be very sensitive to omega 3 fatty acids, with a dose of around 2g per day reducing it significantly ④. These kinds of doses would come from supplementation. (See page 58 for recommendations.) My approach—and my advice to you—is to eat fish and plenty of it and take supplements, too. Omega 3 fatty acids have also been shown both to deliver a dose dependent (that is, greater intake = greater result) reduction in blood pressure ⑤, and to reduce clotting factors that may offer some protection against thrombus formation ⑥.

THE BALANCING ACT

So, as you can see, omega 3 fatty acids are a pretty important part of the picture, while too much omega 6 can cause a problem. So it is therefore vital that we get the balance right. With the current trends arising from research, the recommendation now is to aim for a 2:1

ratio in favor of omega 3. That basically means that you need to be eating twice as much omega 3 as omega 6 in order to maximize the potential benefits, and counteract any negative effects of omega 6 in the body. Thankfully, this is pretty easy to manage in practice.

The first step is to avoid most vegetable oils like the plague. These are the so-called "heart-healthy" oils such as sunflower oil, corn oil, or the generic vegetable oil. These are basically pure omega 6 and will send your levels rocketing up very fast.

In place of these oils there are two cooking oils to choose from. In most of my cooking I use olive oil. The dominant fatty acid in olive oil is something called oleic acid which comes into a third category: omega 9. Omega 9 fatty acids have zero influence on omega balance, so don't particularly present a problem at all.

The other oil I use is coconut oil. This is best for high temperature cooking as it is completely heat stable. Also the fatty acids found in there, medium chain triglycerides, are rapidly broken down and used as an energy source, so their impact on postprandial lipemia (elevation of blood fats after a meal) is minimal.

The next step in aiming for omega balance is to drastically cut back on processed foods. This is good advice for a million and one reasons but, in terms of omega balance, many processed foods use untold amounts of vegetable oils. They are very cheap and, for decades, food manufacturers have been under pressure to reduce saturated fat in foods, so have moved over to cheap vegetable oils as an alternative. Most ready meals, premade sauces, cookies, cakes, and so on will have a lot of omega 6 in them. Get back to basics, as we do in the recipes in this book, and get cooking from scratch as much as you can.

The second part of the solution is to up the levels of omega 3 in your diet. The first and most obvious place to start is by making sure you eat oily fish around three times every week. Then you could also consider taking supplements. I personally take an omega 3 supplement that contains 750mg of EPA and 250mg of DHA twice daily. (But if you are taking medication such as warfarin, or if you have recently had a heparin injection, please check with your physician before using high-dose fish oil supplements as there is potential for interaction here.)

KNOW YOUR NUMBERS

For those of you that really want to be serious about getting your omega balance in check, there is now a home test available online that you can carry out which essentially tells you the ratio between omega 3 and omega 6 in your tissues.

THE GLYCEMIC RESPONSE OF FOODS

One area that is very often overlooked in cardiovascular health is the glycemic response of foods. This basically describes the rate and extent to which a food raises our blood sugar. Different foods, because of their composition, will release their energy at different rates. Pure glucose, for example, will send blood sugar up very rapidly and vigorously. Glucose is actually the benchmark against which all other foods are measured. It is the simplest form of sugar, so requires no digestive effort. It is consumed, then goes straight into circulation.

Foods vary in their make up and complexity and certain factors will influence how rapidly foods release their energy. Fiber is one of the biggest factors. Let's compare white and brown bread, for example. Brown bread has all the fiber from the wheat husk and many brown breads have additional seeds and fibers added to them. White bread, on the other hand, has had all of the wheat husks removed and so the fiber content is drastically lower. The fiber in the brown bread will simply make the sugars in the bread harder to get to and will require more digestive effort to release. With the refined white bread, on the other hand, the lack of fiber makes the sugar much easier to get at. In the higher fiber food, the sugar is released at a more slow and steady pace, whereas with refined foods (anything white is usually a culprit) it is released at a very rapid pace as it takes far less digestive effort in the digestive tract to liberate the easy-to-get-at glucose.

Another influence on glycemic response is the combinations in which you eat certain foods. Adding protein to your carbohydrates, for example, will require a great deal more digestive effort to liberate the glucose. This is because proteins are digested more slowly, so there is a lot more work for the digestive system to do when you eat a combination of protein and carbohydrate. The end result is that you will get a slow, even drip-feeding of glucose into the bloodstream, rather than the giant surge you get when eating refined carbohydrates.

But why does any of this matter? Well, an obvious reason is that it will greatly influence your energy levels and mood stability, but that is by the by for your heart, which is what we are concerned with in this book. The glycemic response of your diet over the long term is of great importance to cardiovascular health.

When our blood sugar rises, our bodies secrete a hormone called insulin. This hormone basically tells our cells to take in glucose for converting into a substance called ATP, the energy unit that cells run off. So, the first reason insulin is secreted is so that the cells know there is glucose available for use. But the other factor to consider is that our blood sugar must stay at a very precise level. If it gets too high or too low, both states are potentially life threatening. In light of this, there are very precise balance homeostatic (homeostasis = the physiological control of balance in the body) mechanisms in place that control blood sugar. If it drops too low, the secretion of hormones that stimulate appetite is upregulated. Another hormone called glucagon is secreted from the pancreas which encourages the body to release glycogen, the storage form of glucose, for immediate use. If blood sugar gets too high, insulin production goes up, so at the same time our cells' uptake of sugar increases.

However, this is where things can begin to go awry. Our cells only have a certain capacity for how much glucose they can take up at any given time, because if they take in more than they can readily metabolize and change into ATP, what is left over can oxidize and cause damage inside the cell. They can get full. If our cells are full to capacity and our blood sugar remains high, the excess sugar must be dealt with somehow and got out of the system as painlessly and effectively as possible before it does damage.

After filling cells up to their maximum with glucose, the next most satisfactory way of dealing with it is via a reaction called de novo lipogenesis. This is where the glucose gets converted into a fatty substance called triacylglycerol, a fat that can be taken to the adipose tissue (our bodies' fat cells) for storage and taken away as rapidly as possible.

Another word for triacylglycerol is triglycerides ... Sound familiar? They are often measured during routine blood tests that monitor cholesterol and other cardiovascular disease markers. These are the fats that, when in circulation, are susceptible to oxidative damage which can then cause damage to the endothelium. They also encourage oxidation of LDL, which can further damage the endothelium. Further, they make the LDL particles more susceptible to penetrating the endothelium as in the description of plaque formation (see page 30). The clincher is that insulin also increases the likelihood of LDL oxidation, so you get a double whammy blow here. Higher blood sugar on a consistent basis means more triglycerides plus higher levels of insulin. None of this is good news!

Now if you recall from my discussion of fatty acids above, following the "healthy heart" public health campaigns that arose from Ancel Keys's work, we were all encouraged to fill up on more fruit and vegetables (that's a good thing) and more starchy foods (that's not a good thing). We started eating more and more bread, potatoes, pasta, grains, and so on, every day and at every meal.

Now, before anyone thinks I'm trying to get everyone on the Atkins diet, there is nothing wrong with these foods, but in general in the Western world we are eating way more than we should and, in essence, the balance on our plates is all wrong.

Our preoccupation with fat and the advice to veer away from it and eat more starchy foods mean that we are eating a level that is harmful. These foods can raise our blood sugar notably. Now, once in a while that is no big deal. You will simply send out a bit more insulin, your cells will take in more glucose, problem solved. But, our intake isn't just every now and again.

Let's see if this sounds like an inaccurate or extreme picture: how many people would have cereal and a slice of toast for breakfast? A sandwich for lunch? Then perhaps meat, vegetables, and potatoes—or maybe pasta—for dinner? That sounds pretty common, right? Well, do that every day for a week, a month, a year, and you will soon find your body's blood sugar staying consistently high and more insulin being produced, meaning more lipogenesis, more LDL oxidation, more endothelial damage. Nasty!

This situation is such an easy thing to remedy though, using a few simple steps:

REDUCE YOUR INTAKE OF STARCHY FOODS

OK, so this may sound a bit obvious, but this is the place to start. For breakfast, go for a good source of protein such as eggs, smoked salmon, or kippers. Ditch the cereal most days and, when you are craving cereal, opt for oatmeal, as oats have a low glycemic response (see page 55).

Lunches should be built around a good protein source, vegetables, and salads. One of my lunch staples is salmon salad with a bit of feta and an olive oil-based dressing.

The evening meal is one where you can afford to have a bit of carbohydrate, as the carbs help the brain to take up the amino acid tryptophan, which helps us sleep. But this doesn't mean scoffing a bowl of pasta or a big baked potato. Instead, go for choices such as roasted squash or sweet potato. Maybe add some high-protein quinoa or fiber-filled bulgur wheat, or brown rice. These are all very low-GI options and will fill you up and satisfy your appetite. Still, I would advise you only have a very small portion.

WHEN YOU HAVE CARBS, ALSO HAVE PROTEIN AND FAT

This is one of the real keys to buffering the effects of the carbohydrates on blood sugar as much as possible. Both protein and fat really slow down the digestion of a meal, meaning that available sugar will be freed slowly and blood sugar will be drip-fed. This is really easy in practice. You could have poached egg and avocado on toast (delicious, trust me). Maybe a piece of broiled fish with roasted sweet potato and some buttered greens. It truly is pretty straightforward.

By making these simple changes, you prevent the blood sugar roller coaster that, aside from making you feel rubbish, can completely destroy your long-term health. From damaging your cardiovascular system, to causing long-term insulin resistance. See my book *Eat Your Way to Managing Diabetes* to see how this starch-laden diet that dominates the West is causing an epidemic of type-2 diabetes.

DIETARY FIBER

While we are on the subject of such foods, I wanted to add a little note on dietary fiber. We have all heard of the importance of dietary fiber. It is obviously beneficial for digestive health, but we won't go into that now, because there are also many benefits for what we are concerned with here: the cardiovascular system.

Now, due to the conundrums surrounding cholesterol, I am sitting on the fence and watching what happens with the evidence as it unfolds. But, for many, lowering cholesterol is an important goal and until I can be more certain about what the evidence is really telling us, I won't argue against that, despite what my own personal convictions may be. Well, dietary fiber is a useful tool here. As we have already discussed, cholesterol is made in the body naturally. A small amount of this cholesterol leaves the liver and goes straight into circulation. Most of it, however, takes a bit of a scenic route. It is released from the liver with bile, where it enters the digestive tract. Once it gets in there, it is then reabsorbed back into the circulation.

Certain types of fiber, known as soluble fiber, actually form a gel-like substance in the digestive tract which binds to this cholesterol and carries it away via the bowel before it gets the chance to be absorbed. As there is less cholesterol being absorbed, the liver takes more from the blood to make bile acids and for metabolic usage. This takes blood cholesterol levels down. This has been clinically proven with the fiber from oats, a particularly effective soluble fiber called beta glucan. The recipes in this book have a good fiber content and ingredients such as oats are well represented.

THE MAGIC OF MINERALS

We always hear so much about the array of vitamins in our foods. Weird and wonderful fats and fatty acids (guilty) and more antioxidant compounds than you can shake a stick at. However, a group of nutrients that are often overlooked are minerals, some of the substances so vital for human health that even the most tiny microgram difference in intake can be detrimental to our health. In terms of heart health, there are four minerals that are relevant and three of which, if you increase your intake, can have a positive impact on the health of your heart and blood vessels.

SODIUM/POTASSIUM

Sodium and potassium are two of the most important minerals to be aware of in your daily diet, especially when it comes to managing blood pressure. Sodium has been at the forefront of heart health campaigns for many years and rightfully so. We have for a long time been encouraged to reduce our intake of salt. Why? Well, cheap table salts and most refined sea salts are predominantly composed of sodium chloride. Sodium is an important mineral in the body and we cannot be without it. An excess, however, can create real problems in the body.

Sodium has an important role to play in kidney function. Different minerals in different concentrations affect the rate at which fluids move through our kidneys. Sodium basically slows the movement down. When there are high concentrations of sodium in the body, the movement of fluid through the kidneys slows down sufficiently to cause the body to start retaining water. When this happens, the watery portion of our blood, the plasma, begins to increase in volume. This of course increases the volume of blood within the vessel. Which then increases the pressure against the vessel walls, simply because there is more blood in that tight space pushing against it.

Add to this picture the fact that the substance sodium can in itself be vasoconstrictive (cause contraction of the blood vessels, that makes them narrower) and it soon becomes a serious situation, where the risk of endothelial damage or the rupture of a plaque becomes very real.

Potassium, on the other hand, is like the mirror to this. It is a mineral that we certainly don't get enough of, because its common sources are dark green leafy vegetables, and—admit it—these are definitely not top of the list of American favorites. Potassium can speed up the movement of fluid through the filtration mechanism of the kidneys (called the nephron). This can give a diuretic effect and soon begin to reduce plasma volume. In turn, this can take some burden off the vessel walls. The less volume within the vessels, the lower the pressure will be in them, as there is physically less pressing against the vessel wall. Potassium can also help to relax the blood vessel walls, giving a vasodilatory effect.

To reduce sodium intake, do not use table salt and also avoid refined sea salts. A natural sea salt should have a dull, dirty gray color. Refined white sea salts have all the other vital minerals removed and are no better than table salt. One option is to go for a low-sodium/high-potassium salt. There is a subtle taste difference, but when you are using so many fantastic flavorsome ingredients—such as those in this book—you will never know about it and you will benefit your health in a big way. Also, again, avoid processed foods such as ready meals and storebought sauces. These contain untold amounts of hidden sodium. Get back to cooking from scratch as much as possible.

At the same time, increase your intake of potassium-rich foods. The best sources are bananas, sweet potatoes, greens, mushrooms, dairy produce, tomatoes, and some fish, such as tuna and halibut.

MAGNESIUM/CALCIUM

Magnesium and calcium are joined at the hip! Well, not quite, but they do work in tandem with each other all day and all night. This partnership is particularly important in muscle, where they are potent partners in crime. Calcium stimulates muscle fibers to contract, whereas magnesium causes muscle fibers to relax. The two move back and forth, allowing muscles to contract and relax all day. So notable is the effect of these two minerals that they are often used therapeutically. For example, a popular drug for stubborn hypertension is a class of drug called a calcium channel blocker. This reduces the amount of calcium that can get into muscle cells and reduces contraction, in short encouraging muscles to relax.

Magnesium has also been studied as a potential hypotensive agent (something that lowers blood pressure). A 2012 meta-analysis (study of many other studies to determine the significance of results) of 1,173 people found that magnesium supplementation gave a reduction of both diastolic and systolic blood pressure, with the greatest reduction in intakes of over 370mg/day [1].

I feel that supplements are worth considering here. As always, it's all about the food and your emphasis should be on that, but a little extra magnesium in supplement form really wouldn't hurt. (See page 58, for more information.)

In terms of foods, greens are definitely at the top of the list. Green vegetables are rich in something called chlorophyll. This is what makes them green. Chlorophyll has a significant amount of magnesium bound to it by its very nature. So, if it's green, it has got decent levels of magnesium in it. Nuts and seeds, oily fish and beans are other rich sources, but greens definitely rule the roost!

FLAVONOIDS

There are a very exciting group of compounds that are rapidly becoming the new superstars of nutritional research in the field of heart health. These are the flavonoids. They are phytochemicals, biologically active, nonnutrient compounds derived from plants. (When I say nonnutrients, I mean that there is no recognized deficiency disease attached to them. Things such as vitamin C, for example, you can be deficient in. Its intake is absolutely essential for our body to function.)

Phytochemicals, on the other hand, are nonessential. You won't die if you don't consume them. But please don't for a moment think that they are not useful! In fact, when it comes to heart health, I would go as far to say that they are essential. I think they have a vital role to play in a healthy diet.

The richness of phytochemicals in fruit and veg and the power of their activity is part of the motivation behind the five-a-day campaign and a big contributor to the disease protection that is observed in high fruit and veg consumers. Phytochemicals are biologically active, which means that they can directly affect cells, tissues, genes, hormones, enzymes, reactions ... you name it! These compounds literally are like nature's medicine cabinet. There are thousands of phytochemicals in plant foods and many that are being researched for every imaginable aspect of health. But, in terms of cardiovascular health, it seems to be the flavonoids that have come up trumps!

Flavonoids are very broadly distributed phytochemicals, found in almost all plants. In short, they are color pigments and are responsible for colors in plants from yellow and orange, through to deep red and purple. For the most part, flavonoids are known to be powerful antioxidants, helping to protect cells and tissues from free radical damage. However, in recent years, research has uncovered that they may prove to be superheroes in the fight against heart disease. The initial observations here come from meta-analyses of epidemiological data that has, for example, found a correlation between tea drinking and reduced incidence of cardiovascular disease 1. It has been found that there is an average 11 percent reduction in risk for every three cup increase of tea each day ①.

Probably the most well known of epidemiological observations is the curious relationship between wine consumption and heart disease. Many studies have shown that there is an observable dose-related (more intake = greater response, although with wine there is a fine line between benefit and risk) benefit to heart health from the regular consumption of wine ②. This is where the model of the French Paradox came from, the observation that the French, despite a diet high in dairy, meat, and foods high in the saturated fats that were dietary heresy in terms of heart health, had a notably lower risk of cardiovascular disease than did the English, for example ③.

While these observations of association were being made decades ago, it is only in recent years that we have started to figure out how flavonoid-rich foods may actually be delivering their benefits to our hearts and protecting them from disease.

Think back to earlier in this book, when I described the structure of our blood vessels and the role that these structures played. We now understand that flavonoids interact with the endothelium and that is how the above results are most likely achieved.

We know that flavonoids actually get taken up by the endothelial cells. Once inside, they cause a little bit of chaos and act almost like an irritant. When this happens, the endothelial cells begin to secrete higher levels of nitric oxide ④.

If you recall (see page 21), nitric oxide is a powerful vasodilator. The nitric oxide moves from the endothelial cells into the muscular walls of the blood vessel and causes the smooth muscle to relax.

As the muscle relaxes, the vessel dilates and gets bigger. As it gets bigger, the pressure within it drops. Evidence now tells us that consistent, regular consumption of flavonoids can have a notable lowering effect upon blood pressure.

KEY HEART-HEALTHY INGREDIENTS

This is by no means an exhaustive list, but below are some of the everyday ingredients that I think are the real heroes when it comes to keeping our hearts healthy. The good news, too, is that there's nothing obscure here: they are all regular and familiar ingredients that you can find at your local grocery store.

APPLES

This fruit is a very simple, easily accessible, and versatile heart-healthy food. Why are they so good? Apples are very rich in a soluble fiber called pectin. Any of you that make jam will know that pectin is an effective gelling agent. This gel-like soluble fiber will bind to cholesterol in the digestive tract and carry it off before it gets the chance to be absorbed.

AVOCADOS

For years, people thought of avocado as a fattening food. This was back in the days when we were completely obsessed with fat and the merest mention of it would strike fear into the hearts of many. This is, of course, ridiculous. The fats in avocado are unique, amazing for our health, and they should be seen as nothing other than a health food. The fruit is very high in a group of compounds called phytosterols. These are the same compounds that you find in those little cholesterol-lowering drinks. They have been shown clinically to reduce cholesterol, by blocking the absorption of cholesterol through the digestive tract wall (similar to soluble fiber). Avocados are also very rich in vitamin E, which is a powerful antioxidant nutrient. Vitamin E can actually protect LDL cholesterol from oxidation. As we have explored earlier in the book, this can be one of the early factors that triggers endothelial damage, so any protection against this is a vital part of looking after your heart.

BEETS

OK, so I admit that beets are definitely one of those love/hate foods. Personally I am a huge fan and can't get enough of the stuff. Luckily, in recent years it has been found to have many health benefits. One of the areas that has attracted a lot of attention is the effect beets have on blood pressure.

They are very high in natural nitrates, a type of mineral salt. This is then converted by the body into nitric oxide, which is naturally produced to regulate blood pressure. Nitric oxide causes the smooth muscles in the blood vessel walls to relax, which widens the vessels and in turn reduces blood pressure within them. Some small-scale studies have confirmed this effect. This doesn't mean you can throw your medicine in the trash and eat beets all day, though, it just highlights a powerful ingredient that we can consume more of to benefit our heart health.

BLACKBERRIES

Blackberries are incredibly rich in the flavonoid compounds called anthocyanins. These potent compounds are responsible for their deep dark purple color, and are one of the most bioactive flavonoids in terms of stimulating endothelial function. They are known to be taken up into the endothelium, where they can stimulate nitric oxide release.

BLUEBERRIES

Blueberries, like blackberries, are high in the antioxidant compounds anthocyanins. These are the compounds that give them their deep purple color, and have been shown to cause relaxation of blood vessels, protect vessel walls against damage, even reduce cholesterol slightly. Many studies have shown significant benefits to patients with cardiovascular disease, even vascular dementia.

BROWN RICE

OK, it's a health food staple and a lot of people still see it as a bit hippyish, but brown rice has benefits for heart health. It is mostly the high fiber content that makes brown rice useful. It helps move cholesterol out of the digestive tract, reducing the amount absorbed into the bloodstream. It also contains a compound known as gamma-oryzanol, that is linked with reducing levels of bad (LDL) cholesterol.

BULGUR WHEAT

The fiber content of bulgur wheat makes it an ideal ingredient for digestive and heart health, as high-fiber foods will help remove cholesterol from the digestive tract before it can be absorbed. There are also a lot of B vitamins and magnesium in bulgur wheat, which have a soothing and relaxing effect.

This may have knock-on effects for stress-induced high blood pressure, for example. Magnesium also works against calcium in smooth muscle, aiding relaxation and therefore vasodilation.

CACAO/COCOA

Cacao is packed to the hilt with flavonoids. As we have seen, these compounds have been very widely researched and are known to cause the cells that line our blood vessels to release high levels of a compound called nitric oxide, which in turn causes the muscles in the blood vessel walls to relax. When they relax, the blood vessel widens, which reduces the pressure within it. Cacao has been the focus of a great deal of research, with many studies confirming its benefits—albeit transient—for elevated blood pressure and enhanced peripheral circulation (a marker of increased vasodilation). Cacao is also very high in magnesium, which also encourages relaxation of the smooth muscle in vessel walls.

CHILES

Chiles contain a phytochemical called capsaicin, which gives them their intense heat. Capsaicin causes the cells that line the inside of our blood vessels to secrete a chemical called nitric oxide, which as we have seen is naturally produced by these cells (chile just gives them a kick in the right direction). Nitric oxide tells the muscles in the blood vessel walls to relax, so the vessel widens. This has two benefits: firstly, the wider the blood vessel, the lower the pressure within it; secondly, circulation to the extremities is improved. Have you (or anyone you know) turned red-faced after eating something particularly hot and spicy? Well, this is that very vasodilatory response in action!

GARLIC

Garlic has long been championed for keeping the heart healthy. It contains a potent compound—ajoene—which interacts with a compound in the body that regulates the rate and extent to which blood clots. As we have seen, excessive clotting can be a very high risk for cardiovascular incidents, while keeping clotting at a reasonable level may deliver several benefits. Some surgeons even advise their patients against eating garlic before surgery, just in case it increases their bleeding.

On a day-to-day basis, it can protect from clotting, so is a weapon against strokes and heart attacks.

GREEN TEA

Another of those healthy staples. I remember 10 to 15 years ago, when I would drink green tea, that friends, family, all, and sundry looked at me like I'd just stepped out of a spaceship. Well, how times have changed. Green tea has quite the reputation these days as a healthy ingredient, and justifiably so in my view. Green tea has some potentially powerful benefits for the heart. This is thanks to the presence of a group of compounds called catechins. These have been shown to reduce platelet (thrombocyte) adhesion, so may offer protection against clots. There are also other flavonoids present in green tea that can stimulate nitric oxide release and therefore increase vasodilation.

MACKEREL

The omega 3 fatty acids in mackerel have a very favorable effect upon cholesterol levels, and can also protect blood vessel walls from inflammatory damage. Omega 3 also delivers antithrombotic activity and can help to reduce blood pressure. What's not to like? Prolonged regular intake of oily fish, as well as fish oil supplements, has been shown in numerous studies to be associated with a decreased incidence of heart disease and has also been shown clinically to improve several of the clinical markers for cardiovascular disease.

OATS

Oats have become one of the most famous of all "heart healthy" foods today. They contain a soluble fiber called beta glucan. This has been clinically proven to reduce cholesterol in the digestive tract. It does this by forming a gel-like substance, which then binds to cholesterol that has been released from the liver. Once bound to it, it carries the cholesterol out the body through the bowel before it has had a chance to be absorbed back into the bloodstream.

OLIVE OIL

Olive oil has long been known to be beneficial to heart health. The Mediterranean diet is believed to be one of the healthiest ways to eat in the world, and has an exceptional track record for protecting the heart and circulatory system.

One of the main protective elements within that diet is, of course, olive oil. The fatty acids in olive oil have been shown on many occasions to increase the levels of HDL cholesterol, and decrease LDL. Oleic acid, the most abundant fatty acid in olive oil, seems to have a beneficial effect upon blood pressure, with some subtle vasodilatory function.

QUINOA

As I have explained earlier in the book, a high-GI diet is a fast track toward cardiovascular problems. Unlike many grains (which tend to be total starch bombs) quinoa is very, very low in carbohydrates and is very low GI. This means it will release its energy slowly and won't cause blood sugar spikes, making it a perfect alternative to rice for anyone wishing to stabilize their blood sugar more effectively. It also naturally has a high protein content which will aid satiety and slow down digestion of a meal, giving that all-important drip-feeding of blood sugar.

RED LENTILS

Red lentils are another ingredient with a high percentage of soluble fiber. I know I may sound like I am repeating myself a little bit, but I really want to drive the point home. This soluble fiber helps remove cholesterol from the gut, reducing the amount that gets absorbed into the bloodstream through the digestive tract.

RED ONIONS

All onions are amazing for you, but red onions in particular are extra-special for the health of the heart. This is because they are particularly high in flavonoids, part of the cocktail of chemistry that gives them their deep purple color. So, again, these will enter the endothelial cells in our vessels and increase their expression of nitric oxide, aiding vasodilation (widening of the blood vessels), and helping to protect the endothelium from damage.

RED BELL PEPPERS

Red bell peppers are definitely up there with my favorite heart-healthy ingredients. Their deep red color is given by a reasonably high concentration of flavonoids, offering protection to the endothelium and enhancing vasodilation again by—you guessed it—increasing nitric oxide expression by the endothelium.

RED WINE

And you thought it was all bad news, didn't you! Red wine consumption has been shown, in dozens of population studies, to be associated with reduced incidence of cardiovascular disease and many of the clinical markers associated with cardiovascular disease risk. It is believed that this is again due to the flavonoid content and also a compound called resveratrol. Both of these compounds are known to induce vasodilation, have anticoagulant properties, reduce inflammation, and have positive effects upon cholesterol levels. The bad news is ... only two glasses a day.

SALMON

Oily fish are definitely at the top of the healthy heart food chain and are big players in my recipes, as you will see in the next section. Salmon is packed with omega 3 fatty acids, all-important good fats. These help maintain healthy cholesterol levels and protect blood vessels from long-term, persistent inflammatory damage, which can be the first step in the process that leads to heart attacks. Omega 3 is also beneficial for the rate and extent to which blood clots, offering a reduction in clotting.

SWEET POTATOES

Another of my staple ingredients and rightly so, I think. These are packed with anti-inflammatory beta-carotene. This is the thing that makes the flesh orange and which may offer some anti-inflammatory protection when consumed regularly. Sweet potatoes also give a much lower glycemic response than the regular potato, so they are a perfect alternative to fries, mashed potato, the lot!

TROUT

Trout is a fish that has very good levels of the anti-inflammatory omega 3 fatty acids.

TUNA STEAK

Several studies have found that tuna positively affects cholesterol levels. This is most likely due to the high omega 3 levels in fresh tuna. Canned tuna, although it's a great lean protein, is not a good source of omega 3, as all of the oils have already been pressed out and sold (ironically) to the nutritional supplements industry.

REFERENCES

Omega 3:

① Stone NJ. Fish consumption, fish oil, lipids, and coronary heart disease. *Circulation*. 1996; 94: 2337–2340

② Hu FB, Bronner L, Willet WC. Fish and omega 3 fatty acid intake and risk of coronary heart disease in women. JAMA. 2002; 287: 1815–1821

③ Harris WS. N-3 fatty acids and serum lipoproteins: Human studies. *Am J Clin Nutr.* 1997; 65 (5 Suppl): 1645S–1654S

④ Roche HM, Gibney MJ. Postprandial triacylglycerolaemia: the effect of low-fat dietary treatment with and without fish oil supplementation. *Eur J Clin Nutr.* 1996; 50: 617–624

⑤ Howe PR. Dietary fats and hypertension: focus on fish oil. *Ann N Y Acad Sci.* 1997; 827: 339–352

⑥ Agren JJ, Vaisanen S, Hanninen O, et al. Hemostatic factors and platelet aggregation after a fish-enriched diet or fish oil or docosahexaenoic acid supplementation. *Prostaglandins Leukot Essent Fatty Acids.* 1997; 57: 419–421

Magnesium:

① Kass L, Weekes J, Carpenter L. Effect of magnesium supplementation on blood pressure: a meta-analysis. *Eur J Clin Nutr* 2012; 66: 411–8

Flavonoids:

① Peters U, Poole C, Arab L. Does tea affect cardiovascular disease? A meta-analysis. *Am J Epidemiol.* 2001; **154**: 495–503.

② Di Castelnuovo A, Rotondo S, Iacoviello L, Donati MB, DeGaetano G. Meta-analysis of wine and beer consumption in relation to vascular risk. *Circulation.* 2002; **105**: 2836–44

③ Renaud S, de Lorgeril M. Wine, alcohol, platelets, and the French paradox for coronary heart disease. *Lancet.* 1992; **339**: 1523–6

④ Fisher, Naomi DL; Hughes, Meghan; Gerhard-Herman, Marie; Hollenberg, Norman K. Flavanol-rich cocoa induces nitric-oxide-dependent vasodilation in healthy humans. *Journal of Hypertension.* 2003; 21 (12): 2281-2286

USEFUL CONTACTS AND RESOURCES

Organizations

American Heart Association
Probably the best known organization
championing heart health. It offers
a vast amount of information about
heart health, keeping your heart
healthy, heart disease, statistics, and
everything in between.
heart.org

The Heart Foundation
There is lots of interesting information
on their website about how to reduce
your risk of heart disease.
the heartfoundation.org

American Society of Hypertension
As the name suggests, the American
Society of Hypertension is a great
resource for all things high blood
pressure and how to prevent it.
ash-us.org

Nutritional resources

Academy of Nuritrion and Dietetics
There is plenty of information on their
website about how much food to put
on your plate, dietary guidelines,
vitamins, and heart health tips for men.
eatright.org

Nutritional supplements

Viridian Nutrition
This company make an extensive
range of the cleanest supplements
around. Over 180 products including
vitamins, minerals, herbs, oils, and
specific formulae made from the
purest ingredients, with no additives,
nasty fillers, or junk.
viridian-nutrition.com

RECIPES

VITAMIN E
GARLIC (ANTICOAGULENT)
SOLUBLE FIBER
LOW GI

Avocado and poached egg rye toast topper

I concocted this addictive dish one morning when faced with nothing but half an avocado and some eggs in the refrigerator. Oh, what a happy discovery it was!

SERVES 1

½ ripe avocado
1 garlic clove, minced
juice of ½ lemon
low-sodium salt and
   freshly ground
   black pepper
1 slice of pumpernickel
   bread
2 eggs

Scoop the avocado flesh into a bowl and add the garlic, lemon juice, and low-sodium salt and pepper to taste. Mash the avocado mixture and mix well.

Toast the bread while you poach the eggs; the whites should be set but the yolks still runny.

Spread the avocado mixture over the bread, top with the eggs, and sprinkle on a little pepper.

Salmon, pea, and asparagus frittata I am a real frittata freak. They are so satisfying when you are really hungry and are a great way to throw all manner of flavor combinations together. Use precooked salmon (but not canned) from the grocery store, to save time. It's easy to scale up the recipe, as we have done in the photo, to serve more people.

SERVES 1
½ Tbsp coconut oil
2 Tbsp peas
3 to 4 large asparagus
    stalks, each cut into 3
    or halved lengthwise
2 eggs, lightly beaten
1 small cooked salmon
    fillet, flaked
low-sodium salt and
    freshly ground
    black pepper

Preheat the broiler.

Heat the coconut oil in a small ovenproof skillet over medium heat. Add the peas and asparagus and sauté for four to five minutes, until the vegetables have turned a brighter green and are beginning to soften.

Add the eggs to the skillet and cook for a couple of minutes, until the edges of the egg have started to cook well, but the middle is still raw. Add the salmon, low-sodium salt, and pepper and cook for another minute.

Place under the broiler until all the egg is cooked; this should take three or four minutes max. Ready to serve.

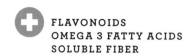

Oat and berry layer This is a gorgeous, speedy breakfast. I find it especially refreshing in the summer months.

SERVES 1
2 Tbsp blueberries
3 Tbsp rolled oats
2 Tbsp blackberries
1 Tbsp yogurt with live
   active cultures
1 tsp flaxseeds

In a tall glass tumbler, layer up the dish: begin with a layer of blueberries, then oats, then blackberries, then oats, and so on. You should finish with a layer of oats.

Spoon the yogurt on top, then finish with a sprinkling of flaxseeds.

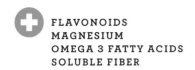

FLAVONOIDS
MAGNESIUM
OMEGA 3 FATTY ACIDS
SOLUBLE FIBER

Mixed seed and blackberry bowl This is a lovely refreshing breakfast. It's a really thick smoothie/dessert/parfait-type vibe.

SERVES 1

scant 1 cup (200 g) yogurt with live active cultures
2 Tbsp blackberries, plus more for the top (optional)
1 Tbsp vanilla protein powder (optional)
1 tsp ground flaxseed
1 tsp sunflower seeds
1 tsp pumpkin seeds

Place the yogurt, berries, and protein powder into a food processor and blend into a thick, creamy, smoothie-type texture.

Transfer to a serving bowl and sprinkle with the flax, sunflower, and pumpkin seeds. You could also place a few whole berries on top for added color, if desired.

Kippers, boiled egg, and watercress salad

OK, so I know having salad at breakfast may seem a bit alien. But in many parts of the world it is the norm and, on my travels, I have become very fond of the idea. Give it a try. Break the mold. You will soon see how refreshing it is, not to mention a great opportunity to get more of the good stuff into your body.

SERVES 1
1 kippered herring fillet
2 large eggs
small bunch of watercress
1 Tbsp olive oil

For packaged kipper herrings, cook (usually boil) according to the manufacturer's directions. If the kipper fillet is unpackaged from a grocery store, broil it for eight to 10 minutes.

Hard-boil the eggs according to how you like them. I prefer an eight-minute egg that is still moist in the center, but whatever floats your boat ... Peel them, then slice.

Arrange the kipper and eggs on a plate, add the watercress, and sprinkle over the olive oil.

Creamy coconut oatmeal

Creamy coconut oatmeal Oats are a great ingredient for heart health, thanks to the presence of the soluble fiber beta glucan (see page 55). Oats and coconut are a marriage made in heaven. Give this one a bash!

SERVES 1

½ cup (50 g) rolled oats
scant 1 cup (200 ml) coconut milk
¼ tsp stevia
3 to 4 drops vanilla extract
1 tsp dry unsweetened coconut

Place the oats, coconut milk, and stevia into a saucepan, pour in 7 Tbsp (100 ml) water, and simmer for five to six minutes, until the oats are soft and a creamy texture has formed.

Add the vanilla extract and dry unsweetened coconut and stir well, before serving.

NITRATES
FLAVONOIDS
SOLUBLE FIBER
MAGNESIUM

Beet, bean, and arugula salad with orange dressing

This may sound like a peculiar mish-mash of flavors ... until you taste it. The orange and beet work beautifully together and the pepperiness of the arugula cuts straight through the middle. All this, plus it is a heart-healthy dynamo to boot. Magic!

SERVES 1

For the salad
2 large or 3 medium
    cooked beets
    (not in vinegar)
1½ cups (400 g) canned
    mixed beans, drained
    and rinsed
large handful of arugula

For the dressing
1 Tbsp orange juice
1 Tbsp olive oil
1 tsp white wine vinegar
pinch of low-sodium salt

Assemble all the salad ingredients in a bowl and mix well.

Whisk the dressing ingredients thoroughly until emulsified.

Dress the salad and serve.

Goat cheese, pomegranate, and olive salad

This just oozes Mediterranean delight, with a fresh but indulgent flavor. Nutrient-dense, flavor-packed, and easy to make. Does it get much better? Pomegranate is now available preprepared, so is also hassle free.

SERVES 1

For the salad
2 handfuls of mixed
    salad greens
2 Tbsp kalamata olives
½ red bell pepper, finely
    chopped
2 Tbsp pomegranate
    seeds
½ cup (75 to 80 g)
    crumbled goat cheese

For the dressing
1 Tbsp olive oil
1 tsp balsamic vinegar
low-sodium salt and
    freshly ground
    black pepper

Combine the greens, olives, pepper, and pomegranate in a salad bowl.

Whisk the dressing ingredients thoroughly until emulsified, then pour the dressing over the salad and toss well.

Crumble the cheese over the top.

Herbed chickpea salad with sundried tomatoes and spinach This is such a flavorful little treat. Easy to prepare, filling, and packed with the good stuff!

SERVES 1
½ Tbsp olive oil,
    plus more to dress
3 handfuls of
    baby spinach
leaves from a few
    sprigs of parsley
leaves from a few
    sprigs of thyme
1½ cups (400 g) canned
    chickpeas, drained
    and rinsed
1 scallion, minced
8 sundried tomatoes,
    chopped
juice of ½ lemon
freshly ground
    black pepper

Pour the oil into a saucepan placed over medium heat, then sauté the spinach for one or two minutes, just until it wilts.

Mix the cooked spinach with the herbs, chickpeas, scallion, and sundried tomatoes. Add a little olive oil, the lemon juice, and pepper, and mix well.

Speedy tomato and paprika soup This is a seriously speedy soup. Canned tomatoes really aren't that bad as long as they are pure and don't have added sugar (just read the label). And oddly enough, when tomatoes are cooked and processed, though the vitamin C may be destroyed the heart-healthy carotenoid lycopene actually becomes more bioavailable to the body! This is a doddle to make and is a speedy lunchtime fix.

SERVES 1
1 Tbsp olive oil
1 red onion, minced
2 garlic cloves, minced
low-sodium salt and
    freshly ground
    black pepper
2 cups (400 g) canned
    chopped tomatoes
1 tsp smoked paprika

Pour the olive oil into a saucepan placed over medium heat. Sauté the onion and garlic, with a good pinch of low-sodium salt, until the onion has softened and is turning translucent.

Add the tomatoes and paprika, bring to a boil, then reduce the heat and simmer for 10 minutes.

Pour into a blender (or use a handheld blender) and blitz into a rich, smooth soup. Season to taste and serve.

Spinach and anchovy pita pizzas Pita pizzas are quick-fix gold. Out the package, whack some bits on, under the broiler, bang ... Lunch. That's what you need!

SERVES 1

1 tsp tomato paste
1 whole-wheat pita bread
8 baby spinach
  leaves, torn
4 to 5 anchovy fillets
1¾ oz (50 g) feta cheese

Preheat the broiler to its highest setting.

Spread the tomato paste over the pita. Add the baby spinach, sprinkling it over. Lay the anchovy fillets haphazardly on top, then crumble over the feta cheese.

Place under the broiler for a few minutes, until the feta begins to brown at the edges, then serve.

Smoked salmon, beet, and minted yogurt wrap This is a wonderful portable lunch and much lighter—with a lower GI—than your average sandwich.

SERVES 1

2 Tbsp natural live
    probiotic yogurt
6 to 7 mint leaves,
    shredded
1 small cooked beet (not
    in vinegar), chopped
low-sodium salt and
    freshly ground
    black pepper
1 whole-wheat tortilla
    wrap
3 slices of smoked salmon
a few arugula leaves
    (optional)

You choose how to assemble this; it's your lunch, after all. You can mix the yogurt, mint, and beet together in a bowl and season to taste, or you can keep all the elements separate.

Place the wrap on a counter and add the salmon, yogurt, mint, and beet in the center, with the arugula leaves (if using), then roll it up.

FLAVONOIDS
SOLUBLE FIBER
CAROTENOIDS
AJOENE

Roasted onion and cannellini bean houmous with vegetable crudités This can be a super-quick option. The onions can be roasted the day before so it is quick to throw together. Or, if you have more time on your hands, they can be done there and then, giving a nice warmer houmous which is an interesting variation.

SERVES 1

For the houmous
1 small red onion,
   thickly sliced
1½ Tbsp olive oil
low-sodium salt
1 garlic clove, minced
1½ cups (400 g)
   cannellini beans,
   drained

For the crudités
2 carrots, cut
   into thin sticks
1 celery stalk, cut
   into thin sticks
4 to 5 whole radishes...
   or any combination
   of vegetable crudités
   you desire!

Preheat the oven to 400°F/200°C.

Place the sliced onion in a small roasting pan and drizzle with about 2 tsp of the olive oil, with a pinch of low-sodium salt. Roast in the oven for 20 to 25 minutes, until the onions are soft and beginning to caramelize.

Place the roasted onion, garlic, cannellini beans, remaining oil, and a pinch of low-sodium salt into a food processor and process into a thick houmous. Transfer to a serving bowl and set in the center of a plate.

Surround with the vegetable crudités and serve.

FLAVONOIDS
MAGNESIUM
CAROTENOIDS

Red cabbage and carrot salad with creamy orange dressing This may sound really bizarre at first but believe me, when you taste it, all will make perfect sense. This is great just as a main course salad, as it's very dense, or is a wonderful side salad for things such as chicken or other white meats.

SERVES 1

For the salad
¼ red cabbage,
   finely grated
1 large carrot,
   finely grated
leaves from a small
   bunch of flat-leaf
   parsley, torn
handful of baby
   spinach, torn

For the dressing
1 Tbsp tahini
2 Tbsp fresh orange juice
1 tsp cider vinegar
low-sodium salt

Combine the grated vegetables, parsley, and spinach and mix thoroughly.

Combine all the dressing ingredients and mix well, before using to dress the salad.

Roasted squash, arugula, and sundried tomato salad This is a gorgeous, colorful, and nutrient-packed salad. It is a perfect lunch when you fancy lots of contrasts in flavor, yet still want something light.

SERVES 1

For the salad
½ small or ¼ large
   butternut squash,
   chopped, skin left on
½ Tbsp olive oil
8 sundried tomatoes
large handful of arugula
1 Tbsp walnuts

For the dressing
1 Tbsp olive oil
1 tsp balsamic vinegar
¼ tsp ground cumin
low-sodium salt and
   freshly ground
   black pepper

Preheat the oven to 400°F/200°C. Place the squash on a baking sheet, drizzle with olive oil, and toss with your hands to coat. Bake at the top of the hot oven for about 30 minutes, stirring occasionally, until soft and roasted and the skin has turned crispy.

Combine the squash with all the other salad ingredients.

Whisk the dressing ingredients thoroughly until emulsified.

Dress the salad and toss well.

NITRATES
FLAVONOIDS
AJOENE

Bold beet and horseradish soup This is an awesome soup with a real bolshy flavor.

SERVES 1 TO 2
1 Tbsp olive oil
1 large red onion, minced
2 garlic cloves, minced
good pinch of low-
 sodium salt
3 large raw beets,
 skins on, chopped
up to 4½ cups (1 liter)
 vegetable broth
2 Tbsp horseradish sauce

Pour the olive oil into a large saucepan placed over medium heat. Sauté the onion and garlic with the low-sodium salt, until the onion is nicely softened.

Add the beets and pour in just enough vegetable broth to cover. Let simmer for about 30 minutes, until the beets are tender to the point of a knife.

Transfer to a blender (or use a handheld blender). Add the horseradish sauce, then blend into a smooth soup.

RUTIN
ERITADENINE
FLAVONOIDS
AJOENE

Soba noodle vegetable stir-fry Soba noodles are an amazing source of the flavonoid rutin, which has been shown to be especially good for the health of blood vessels, protecting the walls from inflammatory damage.

SERVES 1
1 bundle of soba
noodles (they come
ready-portioned)
1 Tbsp olive oil
1 large red onion, minced
2 garlic cloves, minced
1 small chile, minced
1 carrot, cut into
thin julienne
pinch of low-sodium salt
2 scallions,
chopped lengthwise
5 shiitake mushrooms,
sliced
2 handfuls of
baby spinach
3 tsp low-sodium
soy sauce
2 tsp sesame oil

Cook the noodles according to the package directions, then drain and set aside. Pour the olive oil into a small wok or sauté pan set over medium heat. Sauté the onion, garlic, chile, and carrot, with the low-sodium salt, until the onion is soft and the carrot is beginning to soften.

Add the scallions and shiitake mushrooms and sauté for five to eight minutes, until the mushrooms are cooked. Throw in the baby spinach and sauté just until it wilts.

Finally, tip in the drained noodles and mix everything together well with the low-sodium soy sauce and sesame oil.

Roasted sweet potato and coconut soup

This recipe is off the charts in the tasty spectrum. Deep, rich, creamy, and decadent.

SERVES 1 TO 2

1½ large sweet potatoes, skin-on, chopped
1 Tbsp olive oil, plus more to serve (optional)
1 large red onion, minced
2 garlic cloves, minced
low-sodium salt and freshly ground black pepper
1¾ cups (400 g) canned coconut milk
generous 2 cups (500 ml) vegetable broth
cilantro leaves, to serve (optional)
slivers of red chile, to serve (optional)

Preheat the oven to 400°F/200°C. Place the sweet potatoes on a baking sheet and roast at the top of the oven for about 30 minutes, until they have started to soften and the skins are beginning to caramelize.

Pour the olive oil into a saucepan set over medium heat. Sauté the onion and garlic, with a good pinch of low-sodium salt, until the onion just softens.

Add the roasted sweet potato and pour in the coconut milk with enough of the vegetable broth to completely cover the sweet potatoes.

Simmer for about 10 minutes, then blend into a luxurious soup. Serve sprinkled with cilantro and chile and/or drizzled with a little more oil (if using).

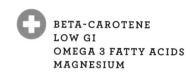

BETA-CAROTENE
LOW GI
OMEGA 3 FATTY ACIDS
MAGNESIUM

Black olive and anchovy-stuffed chicken breast, sweet potato mash, and wilted greens

This is a lovely, strongly flavored dish that is a dinner party favorite.

SERVES 1

1 large skinless
    chicken breast
3 anchovy fillets
4 kalamata olives, sliced
½ sweet potato, peeled
    and chopped
½ Tbsp olive oil
low-sodium salt and
    freshly ground
    black pepper
handful of curly kale
handful of purple basil
    leaves (optional)

Preheat the oven to 400°F/200°C.

Slice a pocket into the chicken breast, cutting into the thickest part. Open up this pocket and add the anchovies and olives, then close and seal with toothpicks.

Place on a baking sheet and bake at the top of the oven for 25 minutes.

Meanwhile, place the sweet potato in a pan and cover with just-boiled water. Simmer for 15 minutes, until tender. Drain and mash with the oil, low-sodium salt, and pepper. Keep warm until the chicken is ready.

Five minutes before you're ready to serve, cook the greens by lightly steaming them until they soften slightly and turn a brighter green. Serve with the chicken and sweet potato mash, sprinkled with purple basil (if using).

Roasted vegetables with quinoa salad

A gorgeous dish that is both filling and light, as well as nutrient packed.

SERVES 1 TO 2

1 large zucchini, sliced
1 large red bell pepper, sliced
1 large red onion, halved, then sliced
drizzle of olive oil
1 tsp garlic powder
1 tsp smoked paprika
low-sodium salt and freshly ground black pepper
generous ¾ cup (150 g) quinoa
leaves from a few sprigs of parsley
1 tsp capers, drained and rinsed

Preheat the oven to 400°F/200°C.

Place the sliced vegetables in a roasting pan with the oil and mix well. Add the garlic powder, smoked paprika, a little low-sodium salt, and pepper and mix again. Roast at the top of the hot oven for about 35 minutes, stirring occasionally so the edges don't catch.

Tip the quinoa into a saucepan and cover with boiling water. Simmer for about 20 minutes, until the grains have softened and what looks like a small "tail" has appeared on the side of each. Drain.

Finely chop the parsley and capers together and mix with the cooked quinoa.

Add the roasted vegetables. Ready to serve.

B VITAMINS
BETA-CAROTENE
LYCOPENE
FLAVONOIDS
AJOENE

Mixed bean chili with baked sweet potato The classic(ish) chili! This gorgeous dish is often served with rice, but following a low-GI diet means that you need to give white rice a really wide berth. (The odd bit of brown rice is fine.) This is a bit of a twist on the classic baked potato with chili con carne. Sweet potatoes have a much lower glycemic impact than regular potatoes, plus are packed with beta-carotene, so are a great option.

SERVES 1

1 sweet potato
½ Tbsp olive oil
1 red onion, minced
1 garlic clove, minced
1 red chile, minced
½ red bell pepper, minced
low-sodium salt and freshly ground black pepper
1½ cups (400 g) canned mixed beans, drained and rinsed
2 cups (400 g) canned chopped tomatoes
1 tsp ground cumin
1 heaping tsp smoked paprika

Preheat the oven to 400°F/200°C. Make a few holes in the sweet potato with the tines of a fork and place in the top of the hot oven for about one hour. Keep checking on it, waiting until it has fully softened.

Pour the olive oil into a large saucepan set over medium heat. Sauté the onion, garlic, chile, and red bell pepper, with a little pinch of low-sodium salt, until the onion softens.

Tip in the beans and tomatoes and bring to a boil, then reduce the heat and simmer for about 10 minutes. Add the spices and simmer for another 15 minutes, until the sauce has reduced and thickened. Season to taste.

Open up the baked sweet potato and spoon a generous amount of chili over it.

NITRATES
AJOENE
FLAVONOIDS
SOLUBLE FIBER

Baked beet wedges with white bean houmous

Baked beet has become like a slightly odd alternative to jacket potato or fries here at Pinnock HQ. It all stemmed from having a large amount of unused beets in the refrigerator that needed eating and a moment of creativity/ boredom. The result was very pleasing indeed. It is too firm to serve whole, but in big baked wedges it is pretty special.

SERVES 1

1 large beet,
    skin-on, cut
    into wedges
2 Tbsp olive oil, plus
    a tiny amount more
    for the beet
1½ cups (400 g)
    cannellini beans,
    drained
juice of ½ lemon
1 garlic clove, minced
low-sodium salt
handful of parsley
    leaves, chopped,
    to serve (optional)

Preheat the oven to 400°F/200°C.

Place the beet on a baking sheet and drizzle with a tiny amount of olive oil. Toss well to coat the wedges. Bake at the top of the hot oven for about 40 minutes, until the wedges are soft, turning occasionally.

Put the beans in a blender with the 2 Tbsp of olive oil, the lemon juice, garlic, and low-sodium salt. Blend into a thick houmous.

Plate up the beet wedges, add a generous helping of the houmous, and sprinkle with parsley (if using). Serve with a green salad.

Squash, goji berry, and red onion soup

OK, fruit in a savory soup. That sounds like I have finally tipped over the edge. But trust me, there is something so special about squash and goji berries. They intensify each other's flavor beautifully. Give it a go. You'll be glad you did!

SERVES 2

1 large red onion, minced
2 garlic cloves, minced
½ Tbsp olive oil
low-sodium salt
1 small butternut
   squash, chopped,
   skin-on
2 handfuls of goji berries
up to 2 cups (500 ml)
   vegetable broth

Sauté the onion and garlic in the olive oil, with a pinch of low-sodium salt, until the onion is nice and soft. Add the squash and goji berries.

Add enough vegetable broth to just cover all of the ingredients, then simmer until the squash is soft and falls apart when prodded.

Blend into a thick, bright orange soup.

FLAVONOIDS
AJOENE
CAROTENOIDS

Balsamic caramelized pepper soup This one is just a bit special. It takes a little time to make but is seriously worth it for the deep, lingering flavor you get in return.

SERVES 1 TO 2

2 red bell peppers,
    seeded and sliced
2 yellow bell peppers,
    seeded and sliced
1½ Tbsp olive oil
2 Tbsp balsamic vinegar
1 large onion, minced
1 garlic clove, minced
½ small sweet potato,
    peeled and chopped
scant 1 to 1¼ cups
    (200 to 300 ml)
    vegetable broth, plus
    more if needed

Preheat the oven to 400°F/200°C.

Place the peppers in a roasting pan and drizzle ½ Tbsp each of the olive oil and balsamic vinegar over them. Roast in the oven for 30 to 40 minutes. Every 10 minutes, take them out, add another ½ Tbsp of the balsamic vinegar, stir, then return to the oven. By 40 minutes, the balsamic vinegar should have caramelized around the peppers and the smell will be divine.

Meanwhile, sauté the onion and garlic in the remaining 1 Tbsp of olive oil, just until the onion has softened.

Transfer the caramelized peppers to the cooked onion, add the sweet potato, then enough vegetable broth to half-cover all the ingredients. Simmer until the sweet potato has softened.

Blend into a smooth soup. If you find it needs thinning out slightly, add a little more broth.

Sweet potato wedges with red pepper-walnut dip An absolute flavor bomb and, though it sounds simple, even light, its nutritional density means it will seriously fill you up. We're talking for hours.

SERVES 1

1 large sweet potato,
   skin-on, cut into
   wedges
2 Tbsp olive oil, plus
   a drizzle for the
   sweet potatoes
1½ large red bell peppers,
   coarsely chopped
½ cup (80 g) walnuts
1 garlic clove
low-sodium salt

Preheat the oven to 400°F/200°C.

Place the sweet potato wedges on a baking sheet and drizzle with a little olive oil. Stir so all of the wedges are coated with oil. Bake at the top of the hot oven for about 20 minutes, until the wedges are soft but with crispy skins, turning them over occasionally.

At the same time, roast the peppers in the hot oven for about 12 minutes. I like to roast them without oil so the skins get a bit charred on the edges and give a beautiful chargrilled flavor. Once they are turning and beginning to soften, remove them from the oven.

Place the roast peppers, walnuts, garlic, the 2 Tbsp of olive oil, and a good pinch of low-sodium salt in a blender or food processor and blend at full power to make a houmouslike dip.

Dip the wedges into the walnut mixture, it is heaven! Serve with a good side salad.

FLAVONOIDS
AJOENE
BETA-CAROTENE
LYCOPENE
SOLUBLE FIBER

Stuffed eggplant This is such a treat, I love all the flavors. Filling, sumptuous, and easy to make. Doesn't get much better if you ask me!

SERVES 1 TO 2

1 Tbsp olive oil
1 large red onion, halved, then sliced
2 garlic cloves, minced
1 large red bell pepper, seeded and chopped
1 large zucchini, sliced
low-sodium salt and freshly ground black pepper
2 cups (400 g) canned chopped tomatoes
1 large eggplant
2 Tbsp rolled oats
3 tsp grated Parmesan

Preheat the oven to 400°F/200°C.

Pour the olive oil into a saucepan set over medium heat. Sauté the onion, garlic, red pepper, and zucchini, with a good pinch of low-sodium salt, for about eight minutes, until they all begin to soften.

Add the tomatoes and simmer for 15 to 20 minutes, until the tomatoes have reduced right down and you have a thick ratatouille. Season further, if desired.

Cut the eggplant in half. Scoop out the flesh from each half, leaving a rim of about ¼ in (0.5 cm) of flesh. Lay the eggplant halves face down on a baking sheet and pour in a little water. Bake for about 12 minutes, until they start to soften. Turn over and bake for another five minutes.

Mix the oats and Parmesan together and season to taste. Spoon the ratatouille mixture into the eggplant halves, pressing it down firmly. Divide the Parmesan topping between them.

Return to the oven for another 12 minutes. Serve with a side salad.

Chicken and tarragon-stuffed peppers with greens

This super-tasty and unusual dish is set to become a favorite. It can work as a lighter dish with a side salad, or as a heartier dinner with sweet potato mash and greens.

SERVES 1

1 large skinless
   chicken breast
½ Tbsp olive oil
1 garlic clove, minced
pinch of low-sodium salt
1 heaping tsp soft cheese
leaves from 2 to 3 sprigs
   of tarragon, coarsely
   chopped
1 large red bell pepper,
   halved and seeded
large handful of
   curly kale

Preheat the oven to 400°F/200°C.

Place the chicken in a food processor and process on a low speed to create coarsely ground meat.

Pour the olive oil into a saucepan set over medium heat. Sauté the garlic, with a pinch of low-sodium salt, for two or three minutes. Add the chicken and continue to cook, stirring and turning the meat, for about 12 minutes, until thoroughly cooked.

Mix in the soft cheese and tarragon and use the mixture to stuff the pepper halves. Place on a baking sheet. Add a small amount of water around the pepper, then bake at the top of the hot oven for 15 to 20 minutes, until the pepper has softened and there is a light golden crust on top of the stuffing.

Five minutes before you're ready to serve, cook the greens by lightly steaming them until they soften slightly and turn a brighter green. Serve with the stuffed peppers.

Chicken and green vegetable nutty stir-fry

This is a great super-quick fix after a long day. A quick-fire, nutrient-dense, one-pot wonder. Almond butter is available from most health food stores and some larger grocery stores. If you can't find it, peanut butter will do fine.

SERVES 1

1 Tbsp olive oil
2 garlic cloves, minced
1 large leek, sliced
1 red chile, minced
1 large skinless chicken
   breast, chopped
1 small zucchini, sliced
handful of curly kale
2 handfuls of
   baby spinach
1 heaping Tbsp
   almond butter
2 tsp soy sauce
1 tsp honey
1 Tbsp slivered almonds

Pour the oil into a saucepan set over medium heat. Sauté the garlic, leek, and chile for about five minutes. Add the chicken and stir-fry for eight to 10 minutes, until it is cooked. (You can cut one of the large pieces in half to check, if you want to be sure; you should see no trace of pink.)

Add the zucchini, kale, and spinach and stir-fry for another five minutes, then measure in the almond butter, soy sauce, and honey. Mix well. Serve sprinkled with the slivered almonds.

Peppered king shrimp skewers with tarka dal

I'm a complete freak for Indian flavors. I find it some of the most divinely flavored food on the planet and, when you push aside those weird takeout staples that have been invented for the Western palates (such as chicken tikka masala), you'll find it some of the healthiest in the world, too. The combination of vegetables, legumes, and antioxidant-dense spices create dishes that are an edible medicine chest.

SERVES 1

1 Tbsp olive oil
½ red onion, minced
1 large garlic clove,
    minced
low-sodium salt and
    freshly cracked
    black pepper
scant ½ cup (75 g) red
    lentils
generous 2 cups (500 ml)
    vegetable broth (you
    may not need it all)
½ tsp ground cumin
½ tsp turmeric
12 king shrimp,
    shelled and deveined
3 wooden skewers,
    soaked for 30 minutes

Pour the oil into a saucepan over medium heat. Sauté the onion and garlic, with a good pinch of low-sodium salt, until the onion softens.

Add the lentils and a small amount of vegetable broth and simmer. As if you were making a risotto, keep adding broth as the liquid reduces, until the lentils are cooked. The finished texture should be like a thin oatmeal. Stir in the cumin and turmeric, mixing well.

Place a ridged grill pan over medium-high heat. Thread four shrimp onto each skewer, sprinkle with cracked black pepper, and place in the grill pan for three minutes each side.

Serve the dal in a bowl with the skewers.

Salmon and beet wasabi stacks This is a rather odd but incredible (and stunning looking) combination that is fantastic as a summer evening dish, because it is served cold. You could also have it as an appetizer.

SERVES 1
2 small cooked beet (not in vinegar), finely chopped
1 Tbsp mayonnaise
2 tsp wasabi
4 slices of smoked salmon, cut into small pieces
juice of ½ lemon
freshly ground black pepper
handful of arugula leaves

Mix the beet, mayonnaise, and wasabi in a small bowl.

In a separate bowl, mix the salmon, lemon juice, and black pepper.

To assemble, place a ring mold in the center of a plate. Put the beet mix in first and push it down well so it is pressed into the shape of the mold. Top with a layer of the salmon, again pushing down well so the salmon takes the shape of the mold. Or you could make more, thinner layers, if you want.

Carefully lift off the ring mold and top the stack with a few arugula leaves.

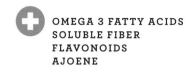

OMEGA 3 FATTY ACIDS
SOLUBLE FIBER
FLAVONOIDS
AJOENE

Tapenade salmon with borlotti bean crush

This is a seriously filling dinner in a hurry, if you use canned beans. It is perfect after a long day at work, when you could eat anything that stays still for long enough. Find black olive tapenade in any grocery store.

SERVES 1

1 salmon fillet
1 garlic clove, minced
1½ red onions, minced
½ Tbsp olive oil
low-sodium salt and
   freshly ground
   black pepper
1½ cups (400 g) borlotti
   beans, drained
1 tsp capers
½ Tbsp black
   olive tapenade

Preheat the oven to 400°F/200°C.

Put the salmon fillet on a baking sheet and place in the oven for around 10 minutes.

Meanwhile, sauté the garlic and onions in the olive oil, with a pinch of low-sodium salt, until the onion has softened. Add the beans to the onion and garlic and sauté for another minute or two. Using a potato masher, coarsely crush the beans; they should be semimashed. Add the capers and mix well.

Remove the salmon from the oven, top with the tapenade, then return to the oven for a final 10 minutes, until the edges of the tapenade get firmer and almost crisp up.

Place the bean crush in the center of the serving plate, then top with the salmon.

OMEGA 3 FATTY ACIDS
MAGNESIUM
AJOENE
OLEIC ACID
NITRATES
SOLUBLE FIBER

Broiled trout with root vegetables and salsa verde This is such a vibrant dish and is awash with fresh flavors and beautiful colors.

SERVES 1
½ raw beet,
   cut into wedges
1 large carrot, cut into
   wedges, or a handful
   of baby carrots
1 small parsnip, cut
   into wedges
2 Tbsp olive oil, or more
   to taste, plus more for
   the root vegetables
low-sodium salt and
   freshly ground
   black pepper
small bunch of parsley
small bunch of mint
small bunch of basil
1 garlic clove, minced
2 tsp capers, drained
   and rinsed
1 tsp white wine vinegar
1 large trout fillet

Preheat the oven to 400°F/200°C.

Place the chopped root vegetables into a roasting pan. Drizzle with a little olive oil, add a generous pinch of low-sodium salt and pepper, and mix well. Roast in the top of the hot oven for about 30 minutes, until they are all soft and beginning to turn golden.

Meanwhile, tip the parsley, mint, basil, garlic, capers, vinegar, and the 2 Tbsp of olive oil into a blender and blend at a slow speed to maintain a coarse texture. Add more oil, if desired.

Preheat the broiler. Place the trout under the hot broiler for 15 minutes, turning occasionally, until a golden crispiness begins to form on the fillet.

Stack the root vegetables in the center of a plate. Top with the trout fillet (or just serve the trout and vegetables alongside), then drizzle a generous amount of salsa verde over the top.

Mediterranean brown rice risotto This is real comfort food and a great way to get the heft and substance you need on a cold winter's evening, without it sticking to your waistline!

SERVES 2 TO 3
1 Tbsp olive oil
1 large red onion, minced
2 garlic cloves, minced
low-sodium salt
1 cup (60 g) sundried
  tomatoes
1¼ cups (250 g) short-
  grain brown rice
2 cups (400 g) canned
  chopped tomatoes
4½ cups (1 liter)
  vegetable broth (you
  may not need it all, but
  it's always best to have
  plenty)
1 zucchini, sliced
1 red bell pepper, sliced

Pour the olive oil into a large saucepan set over medium heat. Sauté the onion and garlic with a pinch of low-sodium salt, until the onion starts to soften.

Add the sundried tomatoes, rice, and canned tomatoes. Simmer until the liquid is notably reducing, stirring very frequently.

At this stage, begin adding broth little and often, topping it off when you notice the liquid beginning to reduce. Keep this up until the rice is virtually cooked.

Now add the zucchini and red pepper and continue pouring in the broth until the rice is cooked and the vegetables have softened.

Whole-wheat pasta with roasted pepper sauce

OK, so as you have probably gathered by now, I'm not a massive fan of heavy amounts of carbs. But we all crave these foods from time to time. Rather than depriving ourselves, we may as well make the best version of these treats that we can. This is a prime example and it just so happens that this sauce tastes awesome! Just saying ...

SERVES 1
1 red bell pepper,
    seeded and sliced
1 yellow bell pepper,
    seeded and sliced
1½ Tbsp olive oil
low-sodium salt
1 large red onion, minced
2 garlic cloves, minced
2¼ oz (65 g) (dry weight)
    whole-wheat fusilli
    pasta
1¾ oz (50 g) feta cheese

Preheat the oven to 400°F/200°C.

Place the peppers in a roasting pan, drizzle with ½ Tbsp of the oil, and a pinch of low-sodium salt. Roast in the oven for about 30 minutes, turning occasionally. This may seem a long time but you want some of the edges to char slightly, as this will give amazing flavor later on. Meanwhile, sauté the onion and garlic in the remaining 1 Tbsp of olive oil, with a pinch of low-sodium salt, until the onion has softened.

Tip the pasta into a pan, cover with boiling water, and boil for 10 to 12 minutes, or according to the package directions. Meanwhile, place the peppers and the onion mixture into a food processor and process into a smooth sauce.

Drain the pasta and stir the sauce through it. Finally, top with the crumbled feta.

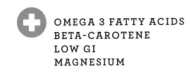

OMEGA 3 FATTY ACIDS
BETA-CAROTENE
LOW GI
MAGNESIUM

Salmon with pea puree and roasted butternut squash

When I first discovered a simply seasoned pea puree it blew my mind. So simple but a real treat. This combination is a regular feature at Pinnock HQ.

SERVES 1
¼ large butternut
    squash, skin-on,
    chopped
½ Tbsp olive oil
low-sodium salt and
    freshly ground
    black pepper
1⅓ cups (160 g) frozen
    peas
1 salmon fillet
mixed salad greens,
    to serve

Preheat the oven to 400°F/200°C.

Place the squash in a roasting pan and drizzle with a little olive oil, a pinch of low-sodium salt and pepper, and mix well. Roast at the top of the hot oven for 20 to 25 minutes, until it has softened and the skins are turning golden and crispy.

Place the peas in boiling water and simmer until soft, but still bright green. If they are dull they are dead! You need them soft enough to semi-puree. Drain and mash with a potato masher, or put them into a food processor and process on a low setting to get a coarse, chunky puree.

Season the salmon with a little low-sodium salt and pepper, place on a baking sheet, and bake at the top of the oven for about 20 minutes, until well-cooked with a crispy skin and marginally crisped edges.

Put a dollop of the pea puree, off center, on the plate, then arrange a stack of roasted squash next to it. Place the salmon on the pea puree and top with salad greens.

B VITAMINS
LYCOPENE
CURCUMINOIDS
AJOENE
LOW GI

King shrimp and spinach curry with herby brown rice A quick, simple curry. It isn't particularly fiery and is very straightforward.

SERVES 2

¾ cup brown rice
1 Tbsp coconut oil
1 red onion, minced
2 garlic cloves, minced
¾-in (2-cm) piece of
  gingerroot, peeled and
  minced
1 cinnamon stick, broken
low-sodium salt
½ tsp turmeric
½ tsp ground coriander
1 cup (200 g) canned
  chopped tomatoes
½ tsp garam masala
½ tsp red pepper flakes
5¼ oz raw king shrimp,
  shelled and deveined
3 handfuls of baby
  spinach
small bunch of chopped
  cilantro leaves
small bunch of chopped
  parsley leaves, plus
  more to serve (optional)
juice of ½ lime, plus lime
  wedges to serve

In a saucepan, cover the rice with just-boiled water and simmer for 25 to 30 minutes.

Heat the coconut oil in a large saucepan set over medium heat. Cook the onion, garlic, ginger, and cinnamon with a good pinch of low-sodium salt, until the onion has softened and the flavor of the ginger has died down a little.

Tip in the turmeric and ground coriander and cook for two minutes, stirring continuously. Add the tomatoes and simmer for 10 to 15 minutes, until the sauce thickens considerably.

Add the garam masala, red pepper flakes, and shrimp and cook for about five minutes, until the shrimp are cooked. Throw in the spinach and cook just until it wilts.

Drain the rice, add the herbs and lime juice, and mix. Serve with the curry, sprinkled with more herbs and lime wedges, if desired.

We've shown it here served with a king shrimp in its shell, which notches the presentation up a gear for a really fancy affair!

Tuna steak with mango salsa, wilted greens, and quinoa verde

A seriously nutrient-packed, fresh, vibrant, and very satisfying dinner. For some reason it reminds me of vacations in far-off places. Maybe that's just me!

SERVES 1
¼ mango, finely chopped
¼ small red onion, minced
¼ small red chile (seeded if you want it less hot), minced
1 tsp white wine vinegar
scant ½ cup (70 g) quinoa
leaves from a few sprigs of flat-leaf parsley, chopped
1 tsp chopped capers
½ Tbsp olive oil
1 tuna steak
large handful of collard greens, or similar

Combine the mango, onion, chile, and vinegar, mix well, and set aside.

Place the quinoa in a saucepan and cover with just-boiled water. Simmer for about 20 minutes, until the grains have softened and what looks like a little "tail" has formed on the side of each. Drain and stir in the parsley and capers.

Set a ridged grill pan over high heat and add the oil. Place the tuna steak on the hot, oiled grill pan and griddle for about three minutes on either side to get a pink middle. If you prefer it more well done, cook for a little longer.

Meanwhile, cook the greens by lightly steaming them until they soften slightly and turn a brighter green.

Plate up the quinoa first, top with the steamed greens, then finish with the tuna and salsa.

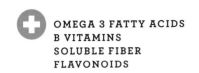

OMEGA 3 FATTY ACIDS
B VITAMINS
SOLUBLE FIBER
FLAVONOIDS

Broiled salmon with red barlotto

Barlotto is basically a risotto made from pearl barley. Barley is a very nutrient-rich grain that is incredibly low GI and full of B vitamins.

SERVES 1

1 Tbsp olive oil
½ red onion, minced
1 garlic clove, minced
½ red bell pepper, minced
low-sodium salt and
    freshly ground
    black pepper
scant ½ cup (75 g) pearl
    barley
generous 2 cups (500 ml)
    vegetable broth (you
    may not need all of this)
1 salmon fillet
juice of ½ lemon

Pour the olive oil into a saucepan set over medium heat. Sauté the onion, garlic, and red pepper with a good pinch of low-sodium salt until the onion and pepper have softened.

Add the barley and a little vegetable broth. Simmer until the broth begins to reduce, then stir in a little more. Repeat this over and over until the barley is cooked and a creamy risottolike texture has been reached.

Meanwhile, preheat the broiler. Season the salmon with low-sodium salt, black pepper, and a squeeze of lemon juice and place under the hot broiler for 10 to 15 minutes, turning halfway through. This should give you salmon that is still a little soft in the middle. If you prefer it more well done, simply cook it for a little longer.

Sea bass with salsa verde and tabbouleh

Fresh, herby, and wholesome. This dish is equally at home on a summer afternoon or a winter day.

SERVES 1
¼ cup (40 g) bulgur
   wheat
1 cup (30 g) flat-leaf
   parsley leaves
3 to 4 mint leaves
5 to 6 basil leaves
1 Tbsp capers, drained
   and rinsed
1½ Tbsp olive oil
1 sea bass fillet
low-sodium salt and
   freshly ground
   black pepper

Place the bulgur wheat in a pan and cover with boiling water. Simmer for around 20 minutes, until it swells and softens.

Place one-third of the parsley, the mint, basil, and capers into a food processor, along with 1 Tbsp of the olive oil, and process in bursts to create a coarse salsa.

Gently fry the sea bass in the remaining ½ Tbsp of olive oil for five to seven minutes, turning occasionally.

Drain the bulgur wheat, add the remaining parsley, coarsely chopped, a pinch of low-sodium salt, and some black pepper, and mix well.

Place the bulgur in the center of the plate, lay the fish on top, then drizzle over the salsa verde.

Chickpea and red pepper stew with sweet potato mash This flavorsome, filling, and wholly satisfying dish is super-convenient and nutrient-dense, with a great depth of flavor.

SERVES 2

1 large sweet potato,
   skin-on, chopped
low-sodium salt and
   freshly ground
   black pepper
1 Tbsp olive oil
1 large red onion, minced
2 garlic cloves, minced
1 red bell pepper, minced
1½ cups (400 g)
   chickpeas, drained
2 cups (400 g) canned
   chopped tomatoes
1 tsp ground cinnamon
1 tsp smoked paprika
handful of cilantro leaves,
   to serve (optional)

Place the sweet potato in a pan and cover with boiling water. Simmer for 15 to 20 minutes, until the potatoes are soft and almost falling apart. Perfect for mashing! Drain, mash, and season.

Meanwhile, pour the olive oil into a saucepan set over medium heat. Sauté the onion, garlic, and red pepper with a pinch of low-sodium salt, until the onion and pepper start to soften.

Tip in the chickpeas and tomatoes and simmer for about 15 minutes, until the sauce reduces. Add the cinnamon and paprika and season further if required. Simmer for another five to eight minutes.

Serve a dollop of the mash with a generous helping of the stew poured over it. Sprinkle with cilantro leaves (if using).

Tuna steak with chile-blueberry compote and roasted celery root

I love this. Tuna steak and fruity sauces are a match made in heaven. Mango is a traditional pairing, but I have made blueberries the star of the show here because of their high concentration of flavonoids.

SERVES 1

¼ small celery root, peeled and chopped
1 Tbsp olive oil
low-sodium salt
1¼ cups (150 g) blueberries
½ garlic clove, minced
½ red chile (seeded if you want it less hot) minced
1 tuna steak

Preheat the oven to 400°F/200°C.

Place the celery root in a roasting pan, drizzle over ½ Tbsp of the oil and season with a little low-sodium salt. Roast for 20 to 25 minutes, until soft and golden.

Meanwhile, put the blueberries, garlic, and chile in a saucepan with 1 Tbsp of water, add a good pinch of low-sodium salt, and simmer for about 12 minutes, until the blueberries burst and the sauce starts to resemble a thin jam.

Pan-fry the tuna steak in the remaining oil for one or two minutes max on each side, or more if you don't want it too pink.

Place the celery root in the center of the serving plate, place the tuna on top, then drizzle the spicy blueberry compote over the fish.

Berry protein smoothie

Berry protein smoothie I have mixed feelings about fruit smoothies. Most of those you can buy are essentially just sugar bombs and can cause many of the issues we covered earlier, when blood sugar levels get too high. But there is a way around that: add protein to the equation. The added protein will slow down the release of the sugars, drip-feeding your blood sugar rather than carpet-bombing it.

SERVES 1
½ carton mixed
   summer berries
   (such as blackberries,
   raspberries, or
   blueberries)
large scoop of vanilla
   protein powder

Place the berries and protein powder into a blender and pour in ⅔ cup (150 ml) cold water.

Blend on full speed into a thick smoothie.

Beet, blackberry, celery, and ginger juice This slightly weird-sounding combination works a treat from both a flavor perspective and also from a nutritional one.

MAKES 1
1 large raw beet, washed,
   skin left on
2 celery stalks
3 Tbsp blackberries
1¼-in (3-cm) piece of
   gingerroot

Run all the ingredients through a juicer.

Nutty chocolate smoothie This simple smoothie has a lovely luxurious flavor, so much so that you may take some convincing that it is actually really rather good for you!

SERVES 1

- ⅔ cup (150 ml) coconut water
- 1 heaping Tbsp unsweetened cocoa
- 1 scoop of low-carb chocolate whey protein powder
- 1 heaping tsp peanut butter

Place all the ingredients into a blender, and blend for about one minute.

I suggest this much time just make sure all the peanut butter is fully broken down. Blenders vary in power, so this amount of time should cover everyone.

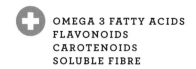

OMEGA 3 FATTY ACIDS
FLAVONOIDS
CAROTENOIDS
SOLUBLE FIBRE

Pomegranate goji omega smoothie This is a great smoothie for days when you want to go a little lighter but don't want to skimp on nutrition. This one is nutrient-dense. I know that pomegranate juice can be a bit pricey in some places, but market demand is pushing the cost down. Shop around and you will get it at a reasonable price.

SERVES 1

⅔ cup (150 ml) pomegranate juice (not anything labeled "juice drink")

1 Tbsp frozen blueberries

2 Tbsp goji berries, soaked in water for 30 minutes to soften, water set aside

1 Tbsp ground flaxseed

Place all the ingredients into a food processor—including the goji berry soaking water—and blend on full power until all the ingredients have blended well.

VITAMIN E
MAGNESIUM

Nutty chocolate avocado pots OK, I know avocado and dessert don't seem as though they belong in the same sentence, but trust me. When making healthy desserts, avocados can be your best friend. They provide a creamy texture without the need to add any nasties ... and happen to be packed with heart-healthy nutrients to boot!

SERVES 2

1 very ripe avocado
1 Tbsp almond butter
1 Tbsp maple syrup, or
   ½ tsp stevia if you want
   to keep the sugar down
1 to 2 Tbsp unsweetened
   cocoa, to taste, plus
   more to serve (optional)

Scoop the avocado flesh into a blender or food processor. Add the remaining ingredients with 1 to 2 Tbsp of cold water.

Process on full speed until all the ingredients have mixed into a smooth chocolatey dessert.

Spoon the mixture into ramekins and chill in the refrigerator for two to three hours before serving, sprinkled with cocoa powder, if desired.

Tonic tipple Surprise ... it's not all about staying on your best behavior. Sometimes we need a little treat. When it comes to heart health, a bit of red wine here and there can be your friend. This summery drink is very refreshing and full of important compounds for heart health, too.

SERVES 1

pomegranate juice
(not anything labeled
"juice drink")
blood orange juice
red wine

Take a red wine glass, fill one-quarter with pomegranate juice, one-quarter with blood orange juice, then top off with a red wine of your choice.

You can add a little ice, too, if desired.

BETA GLUCAN
FLAVONOIDS
OMEGA 3 FATTY ACIDS

Oaty flax berry crumble This is a tasty and simple dessert that takes very little time and is a perfect piece of guilt-free indulgence.

SERVES 1
2 cups (200 g) mixed
   berries
3 Tbsp rolled oats
1 Tbsp ground flaxseed
½ tsp ground cinnamon

Preheat the broiler on its highest setting.

Place the berries and 1 Tbsp of water in a saucepan and set over high heat; the maximum the hottest ring will go on. Stew the berries until they start to burst and, before long, a thicker jamlike texture will form. Place in an ovenproof serving bowl.

Sprinkle the oats, ground flax, and cinnamon evenly over the top, then place the bowl under the broiler for a few minutes until the oaty topping begins to turn golden.

Pears poached in spiced red wine This is a lovely recipe that has a great seasonal festive vibe to it, but is just as at home served cold in the summer.

SERVES 3

1 cup (250 ml) red wine
3 ripe pears, peeled
1 large cinnamon stick
4 to 5 cloves
2 slices of gingerroot
1 tsp vanilla extract
½ tsp stevia, or honey
   if you prefer, to taste

Place all the ingredients in a saucepan and bring to a gentle simmer (not a boil). Cook for 25 to 30 minutes. The pears should be tender to the point of a knife.

Fish out the pears and place in a serving bowl, one per person. Strain the wine through a strainer over the fruits and serve.

Mackerel and caper pâté This is a gorgeous snack. Spread on an oatcake or use it as a dip for raw veggies such as carrots and celery.

SERVES 1

2 smoked mackerel
   fillets
4 Tbsp yogurt with live
   active cultures
1 Tbsp extra virgin
   olive oil
juice of ½ lemon
2 tsp capers, drained
   and rinsed
low-sodium salt and
   freshly ground
   black pepper

Place all the ingredients into a food processor and process at full power until a smooth pâté has been formed.

Place in a bowl and snack at will.

Heart-healthy trail mix

One thing that I hear very often from friends or clients is that they wish they had healthier snacks to hand when they are sitting at their desk. Workplace vending machines are kryptonite to many people, dangling temptation before us, so making your own snacks to take with you is an obvious solution. This little trail mix is tasty, portable, and—most importantly—contains a broad array of heart-healthy nutrients. This makes enough for at least three or four days. Remember, this is for between-meal nibbling!

MAKES 3 TO 4 SNACKS
1 Tbsp pumpkin seeds
1 Tbsp sunflower seeds
1 Tbsp flaxseeds
1 Tbsp goji berries
1 Tbsp dried blueberries
1 Tbsp semisweet
   chocolate chips

Combine all the ingredients together and store in a sealable plastic container.

INDEX

ajoene 54

anchovies: black olive and
anchovy-stuffed chicken breast 90
spinach and anchovy pita pizzas 79

anthocyanins 53

apples 52

arteries 15, 30

arterioles 15

arugula: beet, bean, and arugula salad 71
roasted squash, arugula, and sundried
tomato salad 84

asparagus: salmon, pea, and
asparagus frittata 64

atherosclerosis 30, 31

ATP 42–3

avocados 52
avocado and poached egg rye
toast topper 62
nutty chocolate avocado pots 132

barlotto, broiled salmon with red 122

beans: beet, bean, and arugula salad 71
mixed bean chili 93

beet 52–3
baked beet wedges with white
bean houmous 96
beet, bean, and arugula salad 71
beet, blackberry, celery, and
ginger juice 128
bold beet and horseradish soup 86
salmon and beet wasabi stacks 108
smoked salmon, beet, and minted yogurt
wrap 80

berries: berry protein smoothie 127
oat and berry layer 66
oaty flax berry crumble 135

beta-carotene 57

beta glucan 55

blackberries 53
beet, blackberry, celery, and
ginger juice 128
mixed seed and blackberry bowl 67

blood 11, 13, 17–21, 28, 39

blood clotting 22, 27, 33, 57

blood pressure 17–22, 31, 33, 47, 51–5

blood vessels 15–21, 27–8, 33, 54, 55

blueberries 53
chile-blueberry compote 126

borlotti bean crush, tapenade
salmon with 110

bread: avocado and poached egg
rye toast topper 62

bulgur wheat 53–4
sea bass with salsa verde
and tabbouleh 123

cabbage: red cabbage
and carrot salad 83

cacao 54

calcium 21, 48–9, 54

cannellini beans: roasted onion
and cannellini bean houmous 82
white bean houmous 96

capers: mackerel and caper pâté 138

capillaries 15

capsaicin 54

carbohydrates 42, 45

cardiovascular system 11–16

carrot salad, red cabbage and 83

catechins 55

celery: beet, blackberry,
celery, and ginger juice 128

cheese: goat cheese, pomegranate,
and olive salad 74

chicken: black olive and
anchovy-stuffed chicken breast 90
chicken and green vegetable
nutty stir-fry 105
chicken and tarragon-stuffed
peppers with greens 104

chickpeas: chickpea and red
pepper stew 124
herbed chickpea salad 76

chiles 54
chile-blueberry compote 126
mixed bean chili 93

chlorophyll 49

chocolate: heart-healthy trail mix 139
nutty chocolate avocado pots 132
nutty chocolate smoothie 130

cholesterol 23–7, 30, 39, 43–6
food that reduces 52, 53, 55, 56

clotting factors 13, 22, 31, 39
cocoa 54
coconut milk: creamy coconut oatmeal 70
  roasted sweet potato and coconut
    soup 88
coconut oil 40
compote, chile-blueberry 126
curry, king shrimp and spinach 118

de novo lipogenesis 43
diet 9
dietary fiber 41–2, 45–6
digestion 24
dip, red pepper-walnut 100
dressings: creamy orange 83
  orange 71

eggplant, stuffed 102
eggs: avocado and poached egg rye
    toast topper 62
  kippers, boiled egg and watercress
    salad 68
endothelium 16, 21, 30, 35, 39, 43
  endothelial damage 47
  endothelial dysfunction 27–8, 29
  and flavonoids 50–1, 53, 56
erythrocytes 12

fats 29, 30, 34–9, 45, 52
fatty acids 34–41, 55, 56, 57
fiber 41–2, 45–6
fibrin 13, 22, 31
fish 35, 39, 40, 55, 57
  see also mackerel; salmon, etc
flavonoids 49–51, 53–7
flaxseeds: oaty flax berry crumble 135
frittata, salmon, pea, and asparagus 64

gamma-oryzanol 53
garlic 54–5
ginger: beet, blackberry,
    celery, and ginger juice 128
glucagon 42
glucose 41–2
glycemic response of foods 41–4
goji berries: pomegranate goji

omega smoothie 131
  squash, goji berry, and red onion soup 98
green tea 55
hemoglobin 12
HDL cholesterol 24–6, 56
heart attacks 31
horseradish: bold beet
    and horseradish soup 86
houmous: roasted onion and cannellini 82
  white bean 96

infarction 31
inflammation 28–9, 30, 34
ingredients 52–7
insulin 42, 43, 44
iron 12

juice, beet, blackberry,
    celery, and ginger 128

Keys, Ancel 34–5, 43
kippers, boiled egg and watercress 68

LDL cholesterol 24–7, 29, 39, 43–4, 52–3, 56
lentils 56
  tarka dal 106
leukocytes 12, 30
lipogenesis 44
lipoprotein 25

mackerel 55
  mackerel and caper pâté 138
magnesium 48–9, 53–4
mango salsa, tuna steak with 120
Mediterranean brown rice risotto 114
minerals 46–9
muscles 48

nitric acid 56
nitric oxide 27–8, 51, 53, 54, 55
nuts: chicken and green vegetable
    nutty stir-fry 105
  nutty chocolate avocado pots 132
  nutty chocolate smoothie 130

oatmeal, creamy coconut 70

oats 44, 55
  creamy coconut oatmeal 70
  oat and berry layer 66
  oaty flax berry crumble 135
occlusions 33
olive oil 40, 55–6
olives: black olive and anchovy-stuffed
    chicken breast 90
  goat cheese, pomegranate,
    and olive salad 74
omega 3 37–41, 55, 57
omega 6 29, 36–7, 39–41
onions 56
  roasted onion and cannellini
    bean houmous 82
  squash, goji berry, and red onion soup 98
oranges: creamy orange dressing 83
  orange dressing 71

pasta: whole-wheat pasta with roasted
    pepper sauce 115
pâté, mackerel and caper 138
pearl barley: broiled salmon with
    red barlotto 122
pears poached in spiced red wine 136
peas: salmon, pea, and asparagus
    frittata 64
  salmon with pea puree and
    roasted butternut squash 116
pectin 52
peppers 56
  balsamic caramelized pepper soup 99
  chicken and tarragon-stuffed
    peppers 104
  chickpea and red pepper stew 124
  red pepper-walnut dip 100
  roasted pepper sauce 115
  stuffed eggplant 102
phytochemicals 49–50, 54
phytosterols 52
pita pizzas, spinach and anchovy 79
plaque 30–1, 35, 46
plasma 11, 22, 47
platelets 13, 22, 31
pomegranate: goat cheese,
    pomegranate, and olive salad 74

pomegranate goji omega smoothie 131
  tonic tipple 134
postprandial lipemia 40
postprandial triglyceridemia 39
potassium 46–8
processed foods 40
prostaglandins 34–5
protein 42, 45

quinoa 56
  roasted vegetables with quinoa salad 92
  tuna steak with quinoa verde 120

red blood cells 12
resveratrol 57
rice 53
  king shrimp and spinach curry
    with herby brown rice 118
  Mediterranean brown rice risotto 114
rye bread: avocado and poached
    egg rye toast topper 62

salads: beet, bean, and arugula 71
  goat cheese, pomegranate, and olive 74
  herbed chickpea 76
  kippers, boiled egg and watercress 68
  red cabbage and carrot 83
  roasted squash, arugula, and
    sundried tomato 84
  roasted vegetables with quinoa 92
salmon 57
  broiled salmon with red barlotto 122
  salmon and beet wasabi stacks 108
  salmon, pea, and asparagus frittata 64
  salmon with pea puree and roasted
    butternut squash 116
  smoked salmon, beet, and minted yogurt
    wrap 80
  tapenade salmon with borlotti crush 110
salsa, mango 120
salsa verde: broiled trout with root
    vegetables and salsa verde 111
  sea bass with salsa verde and
    tabbouleh 123
salt 46–8
sea bass with salsa verde and

tabbouleh 123
seeds: heart-healthy trail mix 139
  mixed seed and blackberry bowl 67
shrimp: king shrimp and spinach curry 118
  peppered king shrimp skewers 106
skewers: peppered king shrimp
  skewers with tarka dal 106
smooth muscle 15–16, 21, 51, 53, 54
smoothies: berry protein 127
  nutty chocolate 130
  pomegranate goji omega 131
soba noodle vegetable stir-fry 87
sodium 46–8
soups: balsamic caramelized pepper 99
  bold beet and horseradish 86
  roasted sweet potato and coconut 88
  speedy tomato and paprika 78
  squash, goji berry, and red onion 98
spinach: herbed chickpea salad with
  sundried tomatoes and spinach 76
  king shrimp and spinach curry 118
  spinach and anchovy pita pizzas 79
squash: roasted squash, arugula, and
  sundried tomato salad 84
  salmon with pea puree and roasted
  butternut squash 116
  squash, goji berry, and red onion
  soup 98
starchy foods 44–5
stew, chickpea and red pepper 124
stir-fries: chicken and green vegetable
  nutty stir-fry 105
  soba noodle vegetable stir-fry 87
stress 8, 29
strokes 31
sweet potatoes 57
  roasted sweet potato and coconut
  soup 88
  sweet potato wedges with red
  pepper-walnut dip 100

tabbouleh, sea bass with salsa
  verde and 123
tarka dal 106
tea 50
thrombocytes 13, 22

thrombus formation 31–3, 39
tomatoes: herbed chickpea salad with
  sundried tomatoes and spinach 76
  roasted squash, arugula, and sundried
  tomato salad 84
  speedy tomato and paprika soup 78
tonic tipple 134
trail mix, heart-healthy 139
triacylglycerol 43
triglycerides 39, 40, 43
trout 57
  broiled trout with root vegetables
  and salsa verde 111
tryptophan 44
tuna 57
  tuna steak with chile-blueberry compote
  and roasted celery root 126
  tuna steak with mango salsa, wilted
  greens, and quinoa verde 120

vasoconstriction 18, 21, 47
vasodilation 18, 21, 27–8, 47, 51, 54–7
vegetable oils 40
vegetables: broiled trout with root
  vegetables and salsa verde 111
  chicken and green vegetable nutty stir-
  fry 105
  roasted vegetables with quinoa salad 92
  soba noodle vegetable stir-fry 87
  vegetable crudités 82
vitamin C 49
vitamin D 24
vitamin E 52

walnuts: red pepper-walnut dip 100
watercress: kippers, boiled egg, and
  watercress salad 68
white blood cells 12, 30
wine 50, 57
  pears poached in spiced red wine 136
  tonic tipple 134

yogurt: mixed seed and blackberry bowl 67
  oat and berry layer 66
  smoked salmon, beet, and minted yogurt
  wrap 80

Clare Hulton—we are really cooking on gas now! Amazing work.
Thank you! Jenny Liddle—you are tireless at what you do! Tanya
Murkett—as always, supporting me and putting up with me no matter
what! A big thank you to all the team at Quadrille, Smith & Gilmour,
Martin Poole, and Aya Nishimura. Catherine Tyldesley, Gaby Roslin,
and all of the wonderful people that have supported my work and
career. Ramsay and Candy. Mom and Dad.

Editorial director: Anne Furniss
Creative director: Helen Lewis
Project editor: Lucy Bannell
Art direction and design: Smith & Gilmour
Photography: Martin Poole
Illustration: Blindsalida
Food stylist: Aya Nishimura
Props stylists: Polly Webb-Wilson & Wei Tang
Production: Tom Moore

This edition first published in 2018 by Quadrille,
an imprint of Hardie Grant Publishing

Quadrille
Pentagon House
52–54 Southwark Street
London SE1 1UN
quadrille.com

Cataloguing in Publication Data: a catalogue record for this book
is available from the British Library.

978 1 78713 141 5

Printed in China